Quilting
200 Q&A

Quilting
200 Q&A

Questions answered on everything from popular
blocks to finishing touches

Jake Finch

BARRON'S

A Quantum Book

Copyright © 2010 Quantum Publishing

First edition for North America and the Philippines published in 2010 by
Barron's Educational Series, Inc.

All inquiries should be addressed to:
Barron's Educational Series, Inc.
250 Wireless Boulevard
Hauppauge, New York 11788
www.barronseduc.com

ISBN-13: 978-0-7641-6360-9
ISBN-10: 0-7641-6360-4

Library of Congress Control Number: 2010924139

This book is published and produced by
Quantum Books
6 Blundell Street
London N7 9BH

QUMQ2QA

Project Editor: Samantha Warrington
Production: Rohana Yusof
Photographer: Marcos Bevilacqua
Design: Darren Bennett
Publisher: Sarah Bloxham

Printed in China by Midas Printing International Ltd.

9 8 7 6 5 4 3 2

CONTENTS

INTRODUCTION

I made my first quilt in 1989, quite by accident. After conning my new husband into buying me a sewing machine and teaching myself to make clothing, I saw a quilt on the cover of *Better Homes & Garden* magazine. It was a kaleidoscope pattern, and I thought it would be cool on our bed.

I had never seen a quilt before, ever. At the time I didn't even know that I had quilting ancestors. And I really, really didn't know anything about what kind of fabric a quilt is made from.

I chose to make the quilt from denim (one of my favorite fabrics) and calico. No one was there to explain that the denim was too heavy a fabric to alternate with the lightweight calico. I used scissors and cardboard templates. It was a little hard to machine piece, but I managed it and made a good first effort at matching seams.

But then it was time to quilt the king-sized Beast. With denim on the borders, I tried to hand quilt a rope pattern into the border. That lasted about half a border length. Then, I tried machine quilting the border. No one was there to tell me that we don't machine quilt (remember this was 1989 and the quilt world was just on the cusp of accepting machine quilting as a viable alternative). That lasted one border length. I gave up the idea of quilting the Beast and turned to buttons. I button-tied the center of every block, all 160-something of them. I used comforter-thick polyester batting and a sheet for my quilt backing and, voilà, a quilt was born!

Do I have to tell you that between the denim, the buttons, and the thick batting that this quilt weighs about 40 pounds? I still have it, my testament to beginning quilting, and I'm still just as proud of it, though I won't let it rest on any of the beds in my home today.

That first quilt was all it took. I was an immediate convert to the quilt cloth. I dove into books and magazines. I went to shows, armed with a camera. Quilting was my creative expression, my solace for the years my husband and I lived through our infertility. It was just me and the fabric.

The late 1980s and early 1990s was an exciting time in quilting. Contemporary quilters were stretching beyond the border of patchwork and appliqué. Fabric manufacturers were answering the call for better colors, better dyes, and better prints. Notions companies were exploring ways to make our tasks of cutting, piecing, and quilting easier. It seemed as though the quilt industry changed daily.

What I didn't know, though, was that quilting was also a social passion. I was young, just 21 when I started the

Beast. Absolutely none of my friends quilted. I didn't know about guilds. I didn't even know that the local quilt shop offered classes. I would literally sneak into the back fabric section, buy my yardage, and sneak out. I felt that I was doing something too different and I was afraid to stack up my skills against anyone else's.

I had been making quilts for about 12 years when I became pregnant. I was working as a newspaper reporter for my local paper and I knew I would be staying home with my baby when she came. This change in my schedule gave me the push I needed to walk into my first quilt guild meeting.

I waddled into the Simi Valley Quilt Guild in Southern California one Wednesday night, six months pregnant and nervous as heck. Most of the women were older, which made me feel out of place, but someone around my age stepped up, introduced herself and dragged me to her table where several other women were stitching. And my world became right.

It was at the guild that I discovered the difference between seeing a quilt in a magazine that I loved and seeing it up close, with its maker explaining its gestation. Like fine art, it's hard to absorb the nuances and subtleties of a masterpiece quilt in a picture. Quilts really are three-dimensional, but the depth perception of most quilts is too soft to understand in photos.

I also learned that while I had some skills that needed improvement, many of my basic techniques were fine. My work was better than some, worse than others and that was just perfect. I started taking classes and improving my skills. I learned so much from participating in my quilt guild that, to this day, I credit the guild with my transition from closet quilter to an award-winning professional quilter.

Yes, this needs to be an easy primer for walking through the quilting process. But, I also want to convert you to the fiber-addicted masses. There is something about quilting that draws the practitioner in. Quilters have a great sense of humor and irony. The stories I've heard (and the things I've done) all in the name of our stitching make most people shake their heads with indulgent smiles on their faces. We're a crazy bunch. We love what we do. And there's no limit to your imagination with this hobby.

So I hope that I help you through your early paces in quilting, expose you to enough techniques to keep you interested, and then set you loose in the quilt world to wreak your own creative havoc on us all. Welcome to the club!

ABOUT QUILTING 1

Question 1:
What is a quilt?

In its simplest form, a quilt is a blanket made of three layers: the backing, the batting, and the top. The layers are usually held together by stitching through all three layers. This is the quilting in a quilt.

Typically, the top is made from fabrics sewn together to create a pattern or picture, through patchwork and/or appliqué. But there are many examples of wholecloth quilts, where there is only one fabric used in the top and the quilt stitching becomes the star of the piece.

The word "quilt" can be both a noun and a verb. As a noun, it refers to both the quilt itself and, when we speak of "quilting," to the stitching that holds the quilt together. When used as a verb, to "quilt" refers to the act of making the quilt and/or the quilting stitch.

Modern quilting does not limit the use of quilts to beds and couches anymore. A quilt can be a form of art, displayed on walls for all to enjoy. Quilting techniques can also transform clothing into wearable quilts. Many household items, from placemats to book covers, can also be adapted from quilting techniques.

Question 2:
How old is quilting?

It is surprising to discover that evidence of quilts—in clothing, for decoration, and as bed coverlets—traces back to ancient times! It appears that quilted clothing was used in ancient Egypt, as shown by a carving depicting a king wearing a quilted cloak. Silk quilts dating from 770 B.C. to 221 B.C. have been found in ancient Chinese tombs.

The end of the 14th century marks the date of the first surviving quilts from Europe—three bed quilts featuring trapunto quilting. From that point, quilts and quilting in other items are found throughout Europe, India, Asia, and the Middle East.

A silk patchwork quilt from 1718 was documented by a British family as a family heirloom. The date and the maker's initials were embroidered into the quilt.

A quilt made in 1726 is the oldest surviving quilt in North America. It's currently housed in the McCord Museum in Montreal, Canada.

Immigrants to America brought quilting with them, but it wasn't until the mid-1800s that the craft seemed to take off. Patchwork and appliqué quilts can be found throughout the 1800s. Generally, quilting in the early days of America's history was considered a craft of the well-to-do woman; lower-class women were already weighed down by other household responsibilities. But as fabric manufacturing processes improved, the cost of fabric decreased, making quilting more accessible to the masses.

By the mid-1800s, quilts were an integral part of many households.

The Civil War brought quiltmaking to the forefront of American society as quilts were given to soldiers for their cots and also raffled off to raise money for the war effort. The late 1800s saw an explosion in Crazy quilts, and during the Great Depression of the 1930s, quilt patterns were printed in magazines and newspapers.

With women flooding the workforce during World War II, quilting seems to have taken a back seat to other pastimes and endeavors. There was no great further interest in quilting until the Bicentennial in 1976, when all things handcrafted strode to the front of American awareness and women once again picked up their needles to make quilts. Since then, quilting has evolved into a multi-billion dollar industry, saturating most American homes in one way or another.

Question 3:
What is patchwork?

Patchwork is a quilting technique where pieces are sewn together in a set pattern to form a block. Most patchwork blocks are made from squares, rectangles, and triangles, but there are patchwork blocks that incorporate circles and other round edges also.

Patchwork quilts can have a stunning visual effect—the play between color and pattern work can make a simple design extremely interesting. Many books are available that catalog patchwork block patterns and these can be wonderful resources for designing your own quilts. A patchwork block can vary in size from the very small to the very large, but most average blocks will range from 6 to 14 inches.

BELOW A patchwork quilt adapted from a pattern from "Simple Quilts that Look Like a Million Bucks," by Nicole C. Chambers. The quilt was machine pieced and quilted by Jake Finch.

Question 4:
What is appliqué?

Appliqué is a technique where fabric is cut and manipulated to be shaped and sewn into free-flowing shapes, mostly to create a picture from the finished work.

With the techniques under a quilter's belt, appliqué can be used to create innumerable fabric illustrations, from flowers to complex scenes. In its oldest form, appliqué was used to "draw" folk art shapes, usually of animal or nature scenes. Modern appliqué creates fabric tapestries where the subjects are limited only by the maker's imagination.

Appliqué may be achieved by hand or machine. An appliqué shape may have a finished, turned-under edge, or a raw-edge. There are several ways to accomplish appliqué that are further explored in the Appliqué chapter.

ABOVE Panda and *Floral Delight* *(BELOW)* were made by author and quilt and fabric designer Linda M. Poole.

Question 5:
What are wholecloth quilts?

Popular in France, Great Britain, and other parts of Europe, wholecloth quilts use one main piece of fabric (printed or plain) for the quilt's top. The French have several different variations on the wholecloth quilt, involving different embroidery motifs and stuffing techniques to create dimension to the quilting. It's possible to find preprinted wholecloth quilt fabrics, where you stitch along the printed lines. These lines should wash out when the quilt is complete. This provides a great practice project for hand-quilting techniques.

BELOW Wholecloth quilts were popular throughout Great Britain and offer a wonderful way to highlight beautiful quilting, whether done by machine or by hand.

Question 6:
What are Amish quilts?

Arguably, some of the best known quilts today are Amish quilts. The Amish are known for their simplicity and humility, and these traits are carried into every part of their lives, including their quilts.

As the Amish generally shun anything that could be seen as prideful, Amish clothing is made from simple solid-colored cottons and wools, and in more recent years, polyester. Many of these fabrics are also used in Amish-style quilts, which feature bold, solid colors, simple shapes, and exquisite workmanship. Amish quilts are patchwork; the Amish, until recently, have not incorporated appliqué into their work. In recent years, as the demand for Amish-made quilts has increased their popularity, some simple appliqué work has begun to appear in Amish quilts.

The Amish use their quilts on beds. Often, these quilts are made at gatherings where women work together to assemble and quilt the quilts. But, modern Amish quilters also produce quilts to be sold to consumers outside of their community.

LEFT This gorgeous Amish quilt was made with wool in Lancaster County, Pennsylvania, circa 1900.

Question 7:
What are Baltimore Album quilts?

LEFT A typical Baltimore Album quilt featuring floral blocks.

appliqué picture, often reflecting scenes from Baltimore, Maryland, where the quilts originated in the mid-1800s.

Baltimore was a bustling seaport in the 19th century. Affluent and middle-class women gathered to create Baltimore Album quilts to commemorate events in someone's life.

These delightful quilts started as a form of friendship quilts, where sentiments were written or embroidered onto blocks created by several makers. Each block usually featured an intricate and different

Several talented modern quilters revived the Baltimore quilt movement in the late 1980s and it doesn't seem to be ending anytime soon.

Question 8:
What are Hawaiian quilts?

It's believed that Christian missionaries brought quilting to the Hawaiian Islands in the 1800s, but there is evidence that some form of quiltmaking might have been present in Hawaiian culture even before then.

Hawaiian quilts are defined by

their center appliqué motif, usually created from a single, large folded piece of fabric that is then cut into a large, symmetrical motif often derived from Hawaii's natural habitat. In simple terms, picture when you were a child and would fold a piece of paper into quarters

LEFT Hawaiian quilts, like the example here, are very popular in the quilting community. Traditionally made with one cut motif placed on top of a larger background fabric, Hawaiian quilts are made by hand appliqué. Images used in the designs had cultural significance for the Hawaiian people.

or eighths and cut out a snowflake shape that appeared when the cut paper was unfolded. That's very much what Hawaiian quilting is like.

Once the cut-out shape is placed onto a solid background fabric, it's appliquéd to the fabric and then the quilt is heavily quilted—generally with echo quilting motifs.

Question 9:
What are Civil War quilts?

Quilts played a quiet but important role during the Civil War. Women on both sides of the Mason-Dixon Line made quilts to warm Union and Confederate soldiers. Often, soldiers killed in action were buried in the quilts. Estimates are that about 250,000 quilts were made during this time. Only a handful of Civil War quilts survive today and are mostly housed as treasured items in museums throughout the country.

Most quilts featured simple patchwork patterns that could be

ABOVE A reproduction of a Sanitary Commission Civil War quilt, designed and made by Don Beld of California. Hand pieced and hand quilted.

assembled quickly. Material came from clothing, other quilts, and from whatever supplies were available at the time. Fabric became scarcer as the war raged on. Cotton was grown in the South, but milled in the North, creating an obvious shortage of materials on both sides.

Quilts were also made during the Civil War for fundraising. These quilts were much more intricate and showed off the maker's skills. Album quilts and patriotic themed quilts were popular and could be raffled or auctioned off at fairs and bazaars for money that would then be donated to the war effort.

Today there are tons of resources available for quilters wanting to recreate a Civil War quilt. There are fabrics, patterns, and inspiration abound for the reproduction quilter on the prowl. With the popularity of historical reenactments throughout the United States, fabrics reminiscent of this era can be easily found, as can reproduction quilts.

Question 10:
What are Crazy quilts?

ABOVE Usually made from scraps of fancy fabrics, Crazy quilts often had intricate embroidery throughout their shapes.

It's said that Crazy quilts were a Victorian-era woman's escape from the formality and rigidity of the times. But what's uncontestable is the intricate beauty and distinctive personality found in the typical Crazy quilt.

Crazy quilts were generally made from scraps of the finest fabrics available. Rich velvets, elegant silks, and lush satins were sewn together in random shapes. Then, embroidery patterns and pictures were stitched on the seams and in the centers of the fabrics. Well-to-do ladies of the time competed to use the best materials and the finest threads.

These quilts were shown off on sofas and were not usually found on beds.

Crazy quilts are alive and thriving today. Modern quilters enjoy the handwork involved, the creativity of personalizing the stitching, and the use of fabrics other than cotton for a quilt. There are groups and organizations dedicated solely to Crazy quilts. Many books are available offering Crazy quilt patterns and embroidery techniques.

Question 11:
What is Sashiko?

Sashiko is a Japanese stitching technique where a long running stitch is used to join layers of fabric for garments and other fabrications. The stitches are made with a heavy white thread and the background fabric is traditionally indigo. The stitches are generally longer than is found in traditional hand quilting in order to highlight the beautiful pictures created by the stitches, as well as the accompanying patchwork or other quilt elements.

BELOW Sashiko is a type of Japanese quilting where a heavy white thread is used to stitch shapes onto indigo colored fabric.

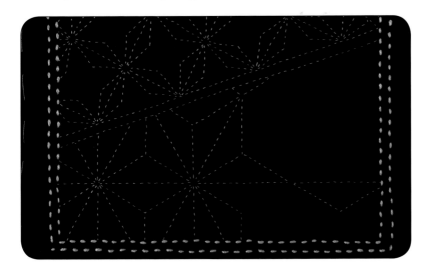

Question 12:
What are Medallion quilts?

American Medallion quilts can be traced back to the late 1700s. A Medallion quilt has a central feature, often created from appliqué that is then framed by a series of complex borders. Medallion quilts are traditional in origination and make great "Round Robin" projects.

Medallion quilts offer a great way to blend patchwork and appliqué in a project. They can be made in any shape.

BELOW A medallion quilt, reproduced by permission of the American Museum in Bath, U.K.

About Quilting

Question 13:
What are Friendship quilts?

A Friendship quilt is defined by the sentiments written on the quilt, either in individual blocks, or throughout the quilt as a whole. There is no defined style for Friendship quilts, but many traditional Friendship quilts feature patchwork blocks.

Friendship quilts can be traced back into American history with surviving examples appearing about a century ago. A Friendship quilt is a delightful gift for someone retiring, moving, getting married, or marking any other milestone in life.

BELOW This example of a Friendship quilt comes from my own collection. Made for me by the members of the Simi Valley Quilt Guild in California, this quilt commemorates the year I served as the guild's president. Many of the guild's members signed this quilt for me. Designed and quilted by Vicki Tymczyszyn, 2007.

Question 14:
What are Charm quilts?

Charm quilts, sometimes called scrap quilts, feature many different scraps of fabrics coming together into one quilt. These quilts can feature one repeating block or design, such as a 1,000 Pyramids pattern, which is made from triangles turned in two directions, but can incorporate two or more different blocks or designs as well.

Some quilt guilds and bees host charm exchanges among members to allow members to gather a variety of small fabric pieces for use in a Charm quilt. By sharing small cuts of fabrics with friends, a quilter's stash of fabrics can quickly grow.

BELOW A Charm quilt made from half-square triangles, pieced and quilted by Vicki Tymczyszyn of California.

Question 15:
What are art quilts?

Art quilters themselves have debated the definition of what they do for years, but let's say that an art quilt is one that reflects a message, statement, or vision, or is a reflection of the artist's inner process. These quilts are usually not made for practical use, but for ornamentation and display.

Art quilters are found in the traditional quilt world and there are also many groups, organizations, and quilt shows devoted just to art quilts.

RIGHT Ebbing Mesas is a wonderful example of an art quilt. Made by Rose Hughes in 2009, Ebbing Mesas features Rose's original appliqué techniques and is heavily embellished. This quilt would never cover a bed and is instead intended to be a work of art. Ebbing Mesas, 27" x 35", www.rosehughes.com.

2
POPULAR BLOCKS

Question 16:
What is a four-patch block?

Probably the simplest of all patchwork quilt blocks, the four-patch block is a square block made up of four smaller squares of the same size with two squares on top and two on the bottom. The four-patch is a great block to use for testing your ¼-inch seam allowance.

RIGHT A simple four-patch block.

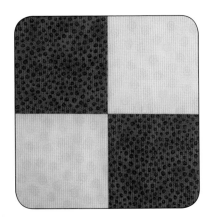

Question 17:
What is a nine-patch block?

Similar to a four-patch, a nine-patch block has three rows of three squares each, like a tic-tac-toe board. The squares' colors alternate from block to block. Many traditional patchwork quilt blocks are based on a variation of the nine-patch block. This is another great beginner's block to work with.

RIGHT A nine-patch block.

Question 18:
What is an Ohio Star block?

An Ohio Star is another very common and well-known quilt block based on a nine-patch pattern. By mixing triangles into the block formation, a star is created. Stars are very popular quilt blocks and are easy to create. There are many stunning quilts that are created using this simple star block.

RIGHT An Ohio Star block.

Question 19:
What is a Churn Dash block?

This variation of a nine-patch block works with a center square and half-square triangles in the corners.

RIGHT A Churn Dash block.

Question 20:
What is a Flying Geese block?

A Flying Geese block is a classic
quilt block that starts as a rectangle
and adds a triangle on two
opposite corners to create an inside
triangle resembling a goose flying
in formation. It's a starting block
for many other blocks and looks
especially good in borders.

RIGHT A Flying Geese block.

Question 21:
What is a Bear Paw block?

This block is made up of half-square
triangles and a small square arranged
around a large square to resemble a
bear's paw.

RIGHT A Bear Paw block.

Question 22:
What is a Rail Fence block?

One of the simplest quilt blocks, a Rail Fence is made from three strips of equal width fabric that are sewn together to form a square.

RIGHT A Rail Fence block.

Question 23:
What is a Wedding Ring pattern?

There are several versions of the Wedding Ring pattern, but most are shown with pieced interlocking curves, which create a secondary pattern of circles and star shapes. A Wedding Ring's construction is complicated and probably isn't suitable for a novice quilter. However, it's a wonderful challenge once a quilter is armed with some basic skills.

RIGHT Wedding Ring quilt.

Question 24:
What is a Storm at Sea block?

This beautiful patchwork block is made up of several triangles, squares, and rectangles. When several blocks are assembled together, there are secondary patterns that can appear in the design, making it look more curved than straight.

BELOW A Storm at Sea block.

Question 25:
What is a Sunbonnet Sue block?

It's believed that this beloved appliqué pattern of a girl with her face obscured by a bonnet first originated in illustrations of children's books around the turn of the 20th century, from several different sources. There are tons of variations for this pattern. A very well-known boy pattern, sometimes called Overall Andy, also exists.

BELOW A Sunbonnet Sue block.

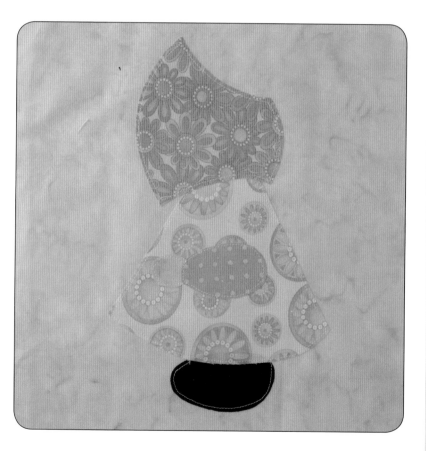

GETTING STARTED 3

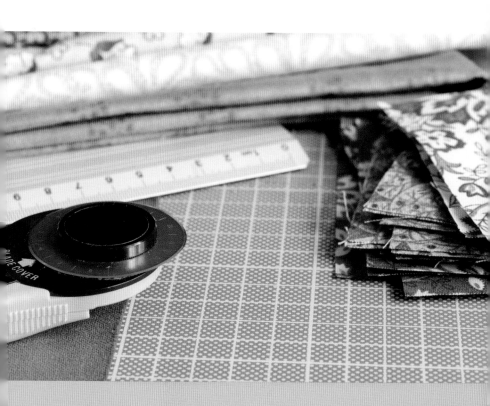

Question 26:
Where do I start?

First, know that as a beginner you can teach yourself to make quilts, but it's always easier with someone to help you along. Check to see if there's a quilt shop in your town that might offer classes, or maybe you have a friend who quilts. Enlist their help. Most quilters are thrilled to pass on their obsession to someone new.

If you're tackling your first quilt on your own, this book is a good place to start when referring to basic techniques. There are also many other books on the market that are geared to beginning quilting. Check your local fabric or quilt shop.

You'll need to decide if you're going to work by hand, sewing machine, or a combination of both. From there, gather your tools and supplies and read the tips below for selecting your first pattern.

Most important, realize from the start that you are learning new skills and you must allow yourself the opportunity to make mistakes. Have patience with yourself. Work on something small at first and commit to finishing the project regardless of the challenge. And remember to be proud of your efforts. You will only get better with practice.

Question 27:
What are the best projects for a beginner to work on?

While the temptation and inclination is to work on a bed-sized masterpiece right from the start, it's unreasonable to expect that process to move smoothly and quickly. Truly, if you're really interested in making quilts, you'll have time for bigger and better in the future, which probably won't be too far forward if you find you enjoy the work.

The best projects to work on as a beginner are simple patchwork quilts no larger than lap size (about 50 inches by 70 inches), which have a plain border and straight setting. Also, it makes sense to make your first quilt by machine rather than by hand. The speed at which you will complete the quilt by machine will become an enticement to work on the next project and the next. Avoid triangles for your first project, as they offer another set of challenges that can be frustrating.

Use a fabric that you absolutely love for your first project as you will be looking at this quilt for a long time. If you use lesser-quality fabrics or colors that you hate, it will take much of the joy away from the finished project.

Lastly, if at all possible, make this first quilt for you and no one else. Quilters are generous crafters and we often earmark that first quilt for a new baby, wedding or some other gift. But, in your development as a quilter, you will very much enjoy coming back to that first effort, looking at what was done right and what was hideous, and relishing in your improvements.

OPPOSITE PAGE These days, quilts can be made by hand, machine or a combination of the two. Most of my quilts are completely made by machine, except for the last step of tacking down the binding pictured left.

Question 28:
What tools will I need?

At its core, quiltmaking can be accomplished with fabric, batting, needle, thread, scissors, iron and ironing surface, and cardboard for making templates. With these tools one could create a hand-pieced, hand-quilted quilt of any size. Of course, quilting has evolved to the point of providing many time-saving tools to make the job easier and sometimes more fun.

A sewing machine is the primary tool that eases the time constraints for the typical quilter. Sewing machines are used to piece quilt tops and they can do the actual quilting. A quilt may be made completely with a sewing machine, or the machine can be used for just certain tasks in the quilt's creation.

Other tools that have revolutionized modern quilting include the rotary cutter, cutting mat, and rotary rulers. I call these the Holy Trinity of Quiltmaking because they have done more to ease the job of today's quilter than any other tools. These tools enable quilters to cut fabric more precisely and quickly than scissors and cardboard templates allow.

As we look at different techniques throughout this book, there will be a tool list included for each technique.

Question 29:
How do I set up my quilting space?

There are three work areas you'll need to set up to quilt successfully: a cutting area, a pressing/ironing area, and a sewing area.

If you're working by hand, your sewing area will become a comfortable chair or sofa with very good lighting nearby. If you're working by machine, you'll require more space and a power outlet for your sewing machine.

When working by machine, the ideal set up is to have your machine sit even to your table top. This ergonomic arrangement eases hand and shoulder tension as you won't be raising your limbs to guide your fabric under the machine's needle. Many sewing cabinets are designed to drop your machine into the top, having it rest on a ledge and creating a flush table-level setting for your machine. If this is not in your ability, don't worry. You can still successfully quilt on your dining table or other surface. You do want to make sure you have enough room to spread out, though, especially as the quilt grows.

Your cutting area's size will be dictated partly by the size of your cutting mat. The best set up allows you to walk around the mat for different cutting angles. A kitchen island is often a brilliant place for your cutting area as it's generally the correct height for standing and you can easily walk around it. Dining tables are also good choices. Again, you need great lighting here.

Your pressing/ironing station can be set up next to your cutting and/or sewing area. This is best as you will be pressing your quilt pieces often. Consider an ironing board placed perpendicular to your sewing area and lowered to the same height as the sewing machine's surface. If you're blessed with a swivel work chair, you can just swing over to the ironing board whenever you need to press the next piece.

BELOW This illustration shows an ideal layout for your sewing area.

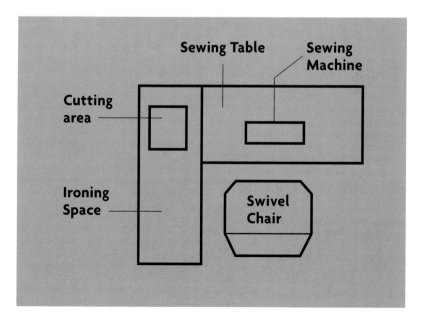

Question 30:
What are the parts of a quilt?

Blocks: The components of the quilt's top. There are thousands of patchwork and appliqué block designs available.

Borders: The strips of fabric sewn around the compiled blocks to create a "frame" for the quilt's top.

Sashing: Strips of fabric used to separate blocks as a design element.

Binding: Fabric used to cover the raw edges of the finished quilt.

Back: The underside of the quilt.

Top: The front of the quilt, usually made from several elements stitched together, such as patchwork blocks, borders, and sashing.

Batting: The soft middle layer of the quilt made from cotton, silk, wool, flannel, polyester, bamboo, or any combination of fibers. What batting is used is determined by how the quilt will be finished and what kind of look the maker desires.

Sleeve: A tube sewn to the quilt's back allowing the quilt to be hung on a rod.

Label: A separate block of fabric sewn to the quilt's back that provides information about the quilt and/or the maker.

Cornerstone: A design element in the quilt where the quilt's borders run into a square—often pieced—in the quilt's corners.

Cornersquare: A cornersquare is used between strips of sashing within the quilt top's design. It's another design element.

Inner Border: A secondary border placed between the main border and the pieced quilt top. A quilt can have as many borders as the maker desires for the design.

Triangles: Traditional patchwork uses many geometric shapes, but squares, rectangles and triangles serve as the base for many patchwork block designs.

Side Triangles: When a patchwork block is set on-point, the top's design will need to use side triangles to "square" up the edges of the finished quilt.

Corner Triangles: When a patchwork block is set on-point, the top's design will also use triangles in each of the four corners, to "square" up the corners of the finished quilt. These will not be the same size as the side triangles.

Alternate Blocks: When a quilt's design uses two different patchwork blocks there is a primary block and an alternate block. Many quilts using two blocks have a secondary design created by the elements of the blocks sitting next to each other.

Question 31:
What are some other quilting terms I need to know?

This is a short list of general terms. There are many more terms specific to certain techniques that will be described in later chapters.

Appliqué: A technique where a smaller piece of fabric is sewn to a background or larger piece of fabric. Together, the smaller pieces can make a picture or design.

Basting: Temporary stitching or gluing used to join the quilt sandwich together in preparation for quilting. Also, basting can be used for some appliqué techniques to prepare the piece for stitching.

Miter: When a corner or binding is created using a diagonal piecing/folding line.

On-point: When a block is turned so its corners point north, south, east, and west in the quilt.

Quilting: The actual stitching that joins the three layers of the quilt together.

Sandwich: When the quilt is layered together with the top, batting, and backing, it's called a quilt sandwich.

Seam allowance: In most quilting projects, a ¼ inch seam allowance is used to join the fabric pieces together.

Setting: How the blocks are arranged in the overall quilt.

BELOW Hand tacking the binding down to the quilt is the most common and effective way to attach binding.

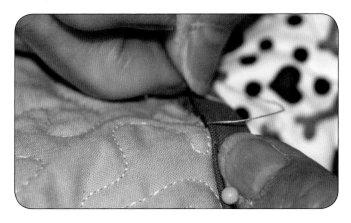

Question 32:
What's the best sewing machine for quilting?

Sewing machines are as personal to the quilter as a car is to the driver. All sewing machines are designed to permanently join two or more pieces of fabric together and, therefore, can usually be used to make a quilt.

The features offered on a sewing machine can enhance your quiltmaking experience and ease the tasks considerably.

Let's assume you have an unlimited budget for purchasing your sewing machine. The best features include:

• Built-in walking foot
• Large sewing machine bed for maneuvering large quilts
• Fast straight stitching speed for when your sewing proficiency allows for speedier stitching
• A zigzag stitch selection for certain appliqué work
• A variety of decorative stitches for different effects on your quilts
• The ability to drop your machine's feed dogs for ease in machine quilting
• An assortment of feet for different sewing tasks
• A needle threader
• A built-in thread cutter
• A built-in light
• An extension table for when you sew-on-the-go with your machine

There is a huge range of pricing when it comes to buying sewing machines and, if you're on a budget, don't hesitate to look at used machines. Sewing machines are sturdy and many people own machines that are hardly ever used. If you're looking at a used model, look for one that has all of its attachments and an instruction book with it. If the book is missing, you can often locate the manufacturer and see if they have any extras. This is a common question and even very old machines from existing companies (think Singer and Kenmore) might have books available. Also, a good sewing machine repairman can fix almost anything.

Some of the most prized machines on the quilt market are Singer Featherweight sewing machines. These small and mighty workhorses offer one of the nicest and most consistent straight stitches on the market, and these machines have been around for many decades. Newer is not always better to quilters.

If you're buying a new machine, ask other quilters about the machines they own and recommend. Use the Internet to do some price comparison online. I'd strongly recommend that you buy the machine from a reputable and local dealer. You want to develop a relationship with this person because you'll be bringing the machine back for regular maintenance and warranty work. Also, a good dealer will understand what you need now from your machine and what you will likely need down the road as your skills improve.

Question 33:
How do I care for my sewing machine?

Most sewing machines require regular oiling and should be brought in for an annual tune-up. Over time and with lots of use, your settings will loosen and it's best for your dealer/repairman to make the adjustments to the machine.

As far as caring for your machine at home, you will need to clean the lint build-up from the bobbin casing and other exposed areas. Quiltmaking creates lots of lint and dust and your machine will attract both in hard-to-reach areas. Most machines come with screwdrivers and lint brushes in the accessory boxes and these are included specifically to allow you to clean the machine. Some newer machines don't recommend that you oil them yourself but others encourage it. Your machine's instruction book will have directions and guidelines for maintaining your machine at home.

EXPERT TIP

66 **Keep liquids away from your machine and, if you have a computerized machine, do not put any magnets near it. The magnets can affect your machine's computer.** 99

Question 34:
What sewing machine accessories will I need?

If you are going to use a machine for even the simplest patchwork quilt, a ¼-inch foot should be your primary investment. As almost all quilt patterns use a ¼-inch seam allowance, a ¼-inch foot allows for accurate piecing of the quilt's fabric.

If your machine does not have a built-in walking foot, consider buying one. A walking foot attachment allows the top and the bottom fabrics to feed under the

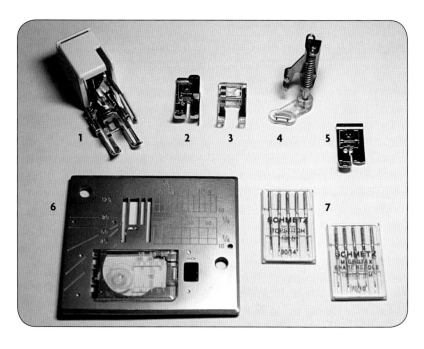

1	Walking foot	5	Single-needle foot
2	¼" foot	6	Single-needle plate
3	Open toe foot	7	Sewing machine needles
4	Darning foot or free-motion foot		

machine's foot at the same pace, helping to prevent puckers and slips. This is especially important when you sew silky fabrics, and also when you're machine quilting using straight stitching.

An open toe foot is helpful to guide stitching that you can see. For instance, if you're using a satin stitch (which is just a very tight zigzag stitch) to finish the edges of some types of appliqué, it will help you to see your progress as you stitch.

A darning foot is another handy attachment. It's used for machine quilting and allows the quilt sandwich to move freely under the needle as you stitch.

Another sewing machine foot that is useful is a single needle foot, sometimes called a straight-stitch foot. This foot only accommodates the needle going straight up and straight down, as opposed to side-to-side. It helps stabilize the fabric better when you're just straight stitching.

If you're going to explore machine quilting, you will also be helped by a single-needle plate. The plate is the metal "floor" of your machine, where the stitching happens. Most standard plates accommodate the needle's full range of motion, as in a zigzag. A single-needle plate, like the foot, only allows the needle to go up and down and thereby stabilizes the fabric better. This one item can make all the difference in the success of your machine quilting.

You will absolutely need extra machine needles. One of the easiest ways to cause skipped stitches in your machine sewing is to neglect to change your needle regularly. We'll look at different types and sizes of needles in later chapters, but for now just know that you will need several on hand.

While this is not generally a machine attachment, you should probably add a true-light to your tool kit that can be beamed down on your sewing machine bed. Ott is one brand that offers small, portable lights that shine directly onto your work area.

Question 35:
What do I need to know about ironing/pressing?

First and foremost, repeat after me, please: "The iron is my best friend."

The difference between a quilter whose work looks fabulous and one whose work is only okay often comes down to the ironing and pressing performed during the quilt's construction.

Your iron can smooth out problem corners, make your quilt lie flat, ease in a piece that's just a shade too small, create crisp points, and so much more.

The most common problem I see in my quilt classes is a too-light touch with the iron. Some quilters seem to be afraid of the iron and they don't apply enough pressure on their work for the iron to make a difference. You need to work that iron and work the fabric underneath.

However, there is no difference between ironing and pressing. Ironing is the act of moving the iron back and forth over the fabric. Pressing is a simple up and down movement of the iron. Most quilters press their fabrics to avoid over-stretching the seams. That's fine, as long as you're using enough pressure to enable the heat to "set" the fabric.

Another great debate in quilting is the use of steam. I, personally, always use steam in my iron, except when I'm working with paper patterns for paper/foundation piecing. That's the only exception. Hot water offers the added force the iron's heat needs to set seams. The use of steam will smooth out most problems from your fabric. And, because you've prewashed your fabrics, you don't have to worry about shrinking with the steam. Oh, and make sure you don't steam the silks. This can stain them.

Generally you'll use a cotton (high) setting on your iron. If you're working with silk, you'll need to lower the setting; synthetics need the lowest settings to avoid melting. You don't have to spend a small fortune on an iron; inexpensive ones can work very well if they can steam. One caution, though, comes with the use of fusibles. A fusible is a glue or other bonding agent applied to interfacings and other materials that, when melted, bonds with a fabric. Fusibles are used to stabilize fabrics, to join fabrics together (as in fusible appliqué) and for other purposes. Each fusible has its own personality and you must follow the directions provided on the packages. Some fusibles will quickly melt and destroy your iron if you don't use a pressing sheet. Others won't work without steam. Some won't work with steam. Always make sure that you never press the plate of the iron directly to the fusible. You will probably end up with an iron that has melted fusing on it forever after.

BELOW Cotton is a wonderful fabric to iron. It's resilient and enjoys a high heat setting.

4 DESIGNING

Question 36:
I want to design my own quilt. How do I start?

First, what or who are you making the quilt for? If you're making a baby quilt, you're looking at a small size. If you're making a quilt for your guest room bed, you'll be sizing it to that bed.

Second, do you have a color scheme in mind or is there a specific fabric you want to use? Again, look at how the quilt will be used. If you're making the quilt for a baby girl you're probably not using "boy" -themed fabrics. If you're making a quilt for a young man going to college, you're not likely to turn to the pink and yellow cabbage-rose prints. Just identifying how the quilt will be used will narrow down your options.

Do you have a deadline for this quilt? It's a common, much appreciated fact in the quilt world that most quilts destined as gifts are usually completed well after the deadline. So don't let a deadline overwhelm you without good cause.

But, knowing how quickly the quilt needs to be completed will help guide the difficulty of the project. If you're just looking to amuse yourself by learning a new skill, then the time factor won't matter. If you're trying to submit your work for a show, time is everything.

Once you have these decisions made, look at your current fabric stash, your budget, and your abilities. Do you want this project to stretch your skills or do you want to get this done? Do you have the fabrics on hand or do you need to heavily invest in materials before starting?

Notice how we're not even hitting the design portion of this quilt yet. We're just getting the logistics down. If you're ready to decide on the quilt's design, start pinpointing your imagination. The rest of the chapter will help guide you through the design process.

Question 37:
How do I choose blocks for my quilt?

There's no set rule for selecting blocks for your quilt, but a fun way to go would be to select blocks based on common settings (four-patch, nine-patch, rectangles, etc.), theme (appliqué, stars), or even the blocks' names.

Generally, the more triangles your block has, the more difficult it will be to construct, especially with small triangles as in Lady-of-the-Lake or Ocean Waves blocks. Also, when you can pair blocks together to alternate in the arrangement, it can be useful to stick with blocks that have the same grid configuration. Indeed, most quilt-block reference books will organize or cross-reference the blocks by the grid arrangement.

Another option is to create a sampler quilt with many different blocks arranged together. You can arrange these blocks in a symmetrical pattern or use different-sized blocks with small filler blocks in between to create more interest in the finished quilt. Many quilt patterns today featuring appliqué blocks use these kinds of arrangement, providing an updated look to a traditional sampler quilt.

LEFT Sampler quilt designed, pieced and quilted by Vicki Tymczyszyn in a traditional medallion style.

Question 38:
How do I sketch out my ideas?

This is the fun part. You do not need a degree in fine art or drafting to work out a quilt idea on paper. What you do need are pencils, crayons or markers, rulers and a compass, graph paper, a sketch book, and a camera—preferably digital.

If you're working with blocks, the job of sketching out your ideas should be easier. But for all projects, you should start with a rough sketch, something to get your ideas down on paper. This is not meant to be pretty. A rough sketch is simply the germ of the idea, something you can refer back to when your memory needs refreshing. Pencil and sketchbook work great here.

Cameras are a perfect tool for capturing "real life" ideas and inspiration. Even if you store your shots on the computer, print out the ones that grab you the most and tape them into your sketch book.

When the time comes to start fleshing out this idea, turn to graph paper. Even if you're working on asymmetrical designs, or on an appliqué quilt not worked in blocks, graph paper provides an excellent way to judge the scale and balance of your design.

If you're working with blocks and traditional settings, you can draw your quilt to scale (an accurate percentage of what the actual design size will be when finished), and this will help you when it comes time to calculate fabric yardage and cutting needs.

Commonly found graph paper comes in four squares per inch, five squares per inch, and ten squares per inch. It also comes in a range of paper sizes from the standard 8 inches by 11 inches and up. I suggest that you have on hand a standard-size pad and an extra-large pad. You can always tape sections together (tape on the back of the page) to make larger or actual-size pattern.

Start by deciding how big your quilt needs to be and then determine how big your blocks should be. The bigger the block, the fewer you have to make, but the effect of using big blocks is very different than what you will get with the same block in a smaller size. Work up an overall quilt plan as well as larger sketches of the blocks and/or appliqué work.

As you draw out your master plan, work only with a dark pencil and graph paper. Later, when you need to try out color schemes, you can photocopy the master plan and use the copies for your crayons and markers. Keep your work together in a file or plastic sleeves because you'll likely be referring back to these sketches many times over during the quilt's creation.

Question 39:
What is composition?

Composition is how a design is arranged when the entire piece is considered. When you look at a quilt, the deliberate choices made by the designer/quilter are the quilt's composition. Composition involves size, color, perspective, texture, balance, overall effect, and the weight of the elements. A good composition employs balance to achieve harmony. Balance does not necessarily mean symmetry.

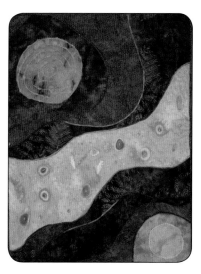

RIGHT This example of composition shows how balance between the quilt's design elements achieves harmony. *Flowing Between Dusk and Dawn*, by Jake Finch, 2003.

Question 40:
What is balance?

Balance is defined by how the visual components (composition) of a quilt work together to create what we hope is a harmonious arrangement.

A quilt that provides equal weight (size, texture, and color) from its elements will most likely appear balanced to the viewer. Symmetry can provide balance to your design.

For a quilt that works with asymmetrical patterns and images, balance is harder to achieve and can be a matter of personal preference. But, when done well, asymmetrical balance is much more interesting in the final design.

Radial balance occurs when a central image is equally surrounded by other images. A square medallion quilt with repeating but differing borders is an example of radial balance.

Balance can be altered or achieved by using variety in the quilt's elements, by creating depth with visual perspective, and through repetition.

As you continue to develop your designer's eye, you'll be able to pinpoint when a quilt is in need of something more or less, or when an element needs to be incorporated.

ABOVE Bounding Through the Woods by Rose Hughes.

ABOVE It's in the Air by Rose Hughes.

Question 41:
What is the rule of threes?

From the story of the *Three Little Pigs* to movie trilogies and three movements in classical music, the number three provides a comfortable framework for creativity and design of all kinds. Quilting is no exception.

Try grouping three of the same elements in a quilt for balance. Three borders in a quilt can also provide a pleasing arrangement just because there are three. Numbers of blocks divisible by three are also safe design decisions for quilts. The rule of three can offer a secure starting place for designing your next quilt.

Another technique is to divide your quilt into three visual segments and watch how this will give balance to your efforts. These segments do not need to be the same size, but they should provide similar weight through color or impact.

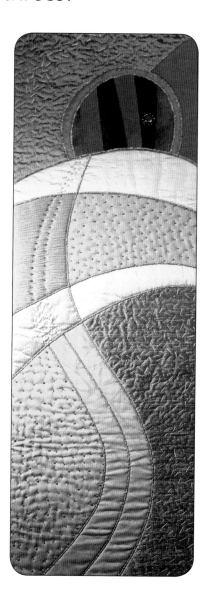

RIGHT In *The Blue Door* by Rose Hughes, the quilt is divided into three sections, each distinct, but harmonious to the whole quilt.

Question 42:
How do I calculate the amount of fabric needed?

The most important thing to remember about calculating fabric is that every piece you cut needs to include the seam allowances in its cut size. For a square that will end up being 4 inches in a finished block, you will need to cut that square at 4 1/2 inches to accommodate the 1/4 inch seam allowances.

Using your calculator, assume that the width of your fabric is 40 inches. Let's work with an example that you can use as guidance.

You are creating a simple nine-patch quilt using a 15-block setting. Each nine-patch block will be 12-inches finished. You will need two fabrics. Each "patch" in the nine-patch will be a finished size of 4 inches square. You will need five patches of Fabric A and four patches of Fabric B in Block One. Block Two will use four patches of Fabric A and five patches of Fabric B.

For Block One (40) total 4 1/2-inch patches are needed for Fabric A. There are (36) total 4 1/2-inch patches needed for

Fabric B. For Block Two (28) 4 1/2-inch patches are needed for Fabric A, and (35) 4 1/2-inch for Fabric B.

Fabric A needs to accommodate (68) 4 1/2-inch patches. Fabric B needs to accommodate (71) patches at 4 1/2 inches.

If your fabric is 40 inches wide, you can cut (8) 4 1/2-inch patches out of each strip. You will need 9 strips at 4 1/2-inches of Fabric A, totaling 40 1/2-inches of the length of Fabric A. In a 36-inch yard, you will need a little less than 1 1/4 yards of Fabric A. Fabric B also needs 9

RIGHT Block One and Block Two for a simple nine-patch quilt.

strips at 4 1/2-inches, totaling 40 1/2-inches of the length. Again, you will need a little less than 1 1/4 yards of Fabric B. Leftover fabric can be used for other projects or worked into the sashing or bindings. Nothing goes to waste in quilting!

If the math stumps you, there are many books and calculators available on the market to help you.

Question 43:

What about computer programs for designing quilts?

There are several excellent computer quilt design programs on the market.

A good design program allows you to create blocks and appliqué images; provides you with a library of blocks; calculates and prints out templates and fabric needs; stores and prints the designs; incorporates fabric scans and provides lots of colors to use in your designs; provides simple and in-depth tutorials; and allows you to create the vision you have in your head for your quilt design.

EQ6 (www.electricquilt.com) (its predecessor EQ5 is also still available in some places) is probably the most popular PC-based program available. It offers fabric images and tutorial books to create intricate and accurate quilt designs. As of this printing, The Electric Quilt Co. only works with Microsoft Windows systems, but some quilters have partitioned their Mac operating systems to load Windows and use their EQ6 program.

Quilt-Pro Systems (www.quiltpro.com) provides several different design programs for both PCs and Macs. Quilt-Pro also provides software that will print out paper foundation blocks from your computer and other printed template papers to be used in your quilt work.

QuiltSOFT (www.quiltsoft.com) also provides design software for both PCs and Macs, as well as additional block libraries.

In the future, there probably will be additional software resources for quilt design. Simply do an Internet search of "quilt design programs" or "quilt software" and you should have several results to research

Question 44:
What about altering an existing pattern?

Sometimes the best inspiration comes from working with what's in front of you and making it more of your own. The only time you need to worry about altering an existing design is if you wish to market that design for financial gain. At that point, you may encounter copyright issues.

Also, if you're working from someone else's design and the quilt is shown in a public venue, it's good form to credit the designer with inspiring your quilt. It would be wrong to misrepresent a design that is partially recognizable as your own.

With all this said, when you're working with an existing pattern, consider rearranging the elements in the quilt; resizing the blocks, borders or sashing; incorporating appliqué or photographs into the work; changing the colors and mood radically from the sample (for example, going from traditional muted earth tones to vibrant batiks will change the feel of the pattern); eliminating blocks to shrink the quilt's size; combining elements from two different quilts to make one; adding embellishments; and so on.

The point is to stretch your creative muscles and allow yourself to put your own stamp on the project. After all, it's your work that goes into the project.

Question 45:
What is copyright?

In the United States, copyright is a legal protection giving an artist/ author the right to protect and benefit from his or her original work for a set period of time. Copyright exists the moment a work is created, but many artists and authors choose to register their copyright with the U.S. Copyright Office with a nominal fee and a formal application. Original quilt patterns, books, and actual quilts are all subject to copyright protections granted to the maker.

Question 46:
Do I need to worry about copyright?

Yes, you need to worry about and respect copyright.

Copyright protects an artist's work. As a quilter, you are also an artist. You would not want your work copied in a way that lessens the value of what you have done. Besides, if you are violating a copyright in your work, you can be legally liable for the artist's loss of potential income. It's rare, but it happens. A copyright violation, called an infringement, happens under specific conditions and can leave the violator open to significant civil action under U.S. copyright law.

The best way to avoid copyright infringement is to not copy or borrow another person's work in a way that will glean financial gain for you; to always credit someone else's idea appropriately and accurately; and to ask for written permission if you do wish to borrow someone's idea.

Here's a classic example of how you might face an infringement problem. You have a beautiful coffee table book of landscape photography. One photo in particular calls to you and you decide to recreate it as similarly as possible in a wall quilt. The wall quilt is only destined for your living room and there will be no financial gain from it. So you copy the photo into fabric and it's gorgeous. You bring it to your guild's show-and-tell and you're mobbed by fellow quilters who encourage you to submit it to a national show. You do, never mentioning the source of your inspiration in the application or artist's statement, and you win a Best of Show award, which comes with a several thousand dollar prize. And, you are approached by a collector who buys the piece from you for their home.

A friend of the book's photographer sees the quilt in a newspaper story, recognizes the image as a copy from the book, and contacts the photographer. Because you've received financial gain from the quilt, at several levels, you have probably just violated the photographer's copyright and may find yourself financially liable for the violation.

No, I'm not an attorney, but copyright infringement is pretty straight forward. If you must use someone else's ideas in a recognizable way, ask them if it's okay.

Question 47:
Where can I find inspiration?

There are so many wonderful places to find inspiration for designing your own quilts.

Look at the world around you. See how nature uses form and light to create beauty. An African violet can be the starting point for both a color board (a selection of colors to use in a quilt) and a design. What about architecture? There's a theater in Hollywood that features plaster reliefs of Art Deco-style carvings. Every time I'm there for a play, I spend more time sketching the details (no cameras allowed) than I do watching the performance.

Pick a style and work a design around it. A contemporary-style

ABOVE A church in Puerto Vallarta, Mexico, by Jake Finch.

ABOVE Fountain at the Adamson House, Malibu, California, by Jake Finch.

quilt is going to look very different from a shabby chic-type quilt. What are the features of both styles and how are they different? Shabby-chic is full of vintage romance, soft colors, tons of flowers. Contemporary style uses hip color combinations and often bold prints. Geometrics are a common sighting in contemporary (and its close sister, modern style) art and design.

Scour decorating, art, and other craft magazines. These publications offer inspiration on every page, including the advertisements.

Instead of turning to visual inspiration, what about using sound for inspiration? If you had to create a quilt based on one of Beethoven's sonatas, what would it look like? What about a pictorial appliqué quilt from your favorite country ballad? Maybe your child or grandchild said something great and you want to capture the concept in a folk art quilt. Do it!

Use whatever you have for inspiration and remember, sketch it or shoot it with a camera to remember at a later time. Inspiration is almost never convenient with its appearance.

Question 48:
What is a design wall?

A design wall is a wonderful tool for assisting in the design of your quilt. Whether you're developing a quilt design as you work or have a bunch of finished blocks and borders that you need to arrange, a design wall allows you the space and perspective to evaluate your work.

Picture a large, flannel board, usually mounted to a wall, on which you "stick" your quilt's pieces. The flannel, or batting, acts as a magnet for cotton fabrics, but also allows the fabric to be repositioned as desired. Many quilters create their own design wall with pieces of foam core board, cork board, or sheets of lightweight plywood covered with flannel or cotton batting.

Even if you do not have enough room to cover an entire wall with a design wall, you can create a folding wall that stores easily, or have a temporary board propped up against a wall as needed. Even a small board will prove helpful in your design efforts.

5
COLOR

Question 49:
What do I need to know about color?

Color is the most important tool a quilter will use. That's a bold statement, but it's true. When you learn the principles of color use, you will be free to experiment in your work.

Many beginning quilters are terrified of color. They see it as a magical trick whose secret they will never know. So they play it safe, working from kits or from a picture of a finished quilt. They can certainly find enjoyment in their process, but they are denying themselves the fun that comes with playing with color.

Regardless of where you are in your color training, pledge to take one or two color risks with your next project. The worst thing that can happen is you won't be happy with the results. But, hey, someone else will be and you'll have a gift at the ready for the next occasion. The information in this chapter will help get you started on your road to color confidence.

Question 50:
What is a color wheel?

A color wheel is a tool used by artists and designers to help visualize color combinations. Color wheels are available in art supply stores, and quilt shops often carry them as well.

Color wheels have a specific arrangement that follows a rainbow pattern. The colors on the wheel are all pure colors—colors at their clearest saturation—without the addition of black, white, or gray colors to change their clarity.

RIGHT Color wheel showing primary, secondary, and tertiary colors.

Question 51:
What are primary, secondary, and tertiary colors?

Primary colors are red, yellow, and blue.

Secondary colors are colors created from equal amounts of primary colors. Red and yellow become orange, blue and red become purple, and yellow and blue become green.

Primary colors mixed with the secondary colors placed next to them on the color wheel create tertiary colors, such as turquoise, magenta, and yellow-orange.

The colors from the color wheel are pure colors—colors that have no mixture of white, black, or gray. These are the most vibrant colors and can lend cheer to your quilt designs.

Color Wheel

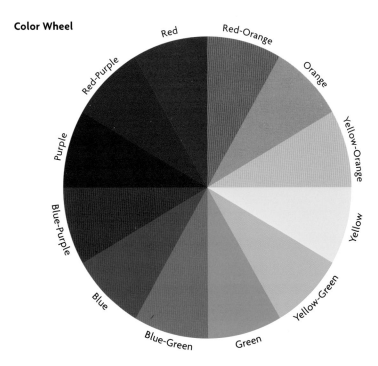

Question 52:
What is hue?

Hue is the word that refers to the color itself. Hue is red, orange, yellow, green, blue, purple, or any colors you can think of.

| Red | Orange | Yellow | Green | Blue | Purple |

Question 53:
What is tint?

Tints are pure colors mixed with white. Pastels are how we normally think of tints. These colors are soft, gentle, and sweet to use.

Blue   Blue with tints of white

Question 54:
What is shade?

Shades are pure colors mixed with black. Even small amounts of black will change a color's appearance, offering more depth and mystery.

Blue   Blue with shades of black

Question 55:
What is tone?

Tones happen when colors are mixed with grays. Soft, muted colors are usually tones. Think of these colors as quiet, or the reflection of winter.

Blue

Blue with tones of gray

Question 56:
What is value?

ABOVE The red value finder is used to determine the value (lightness to darkness) of all fabric colors except for red. The green value finder determines the value of red-colored fabrics.

Value is the term used to pinpoint a color's lightness or darkness. It's common for beginner quilters to work with color to find themselves drawn to medium-valued colors in their fabrics. But it's important to incorporate a full complement of colors in your fabric selections so your quilt will not bore the viewer. Challenge yourself to pick very light and very dark valued fabrics for your quilt, along with the mediums.

The key to successfully using value is to understand that contrast must be achieved within the quilt fabric's values to create interest. If all of your fabrics used are in medium values, regardless of the different hues (colors) used, the quilt will read "blah." Use a range of values in your quilt and you'll be happy with the results. There are special tools, red and green lenses, available that help determine a fabric's value. The lenses help show how light or dark a fabric is when compared to another. These lenses are easily found in quilt shops.

Question 57:
What is a monochromatic color scheme?

First, let's say that all color schemes are just different ways of playing with a color wheel. In a monochromatic color scheme, only one hue is used and is worked with its tints, shades, tones, and values to achieve many different layers of texture and design.

Tints, tones, shades, and values of blue

Question 58:
What is a complementary color scheme?

On the color wheel, colors that are directly across from each other (blue-orange, red-green, purple-yellow) are considered complementary colors, meaning that they enhance each other.

When using complementary colors in a quilt's design, know that using pure colors of each will create an often overwhelming visual affect, (Just think about bright blue and bright orange together and cringe!) The way to work with these color schemes without blinding your viewer is to work with the tints, shades, and tones of these colors. Maybe you have a strong royal blue for one fabric and you use a peach for another. You are still working within a complementary color scheme, but you'll frighten fewer people and still create an interesting quilt.

Blue   Orange

Red   Green

Yellow   Purple

Question 59:
What is an analogous color scheme?

An analogous color scheme uses two or more colors that are next to each other on the color wheel. Picture a quilt made with the range of colors from yellow to orange.

With all of the different shades, tints, tones, and values available to work with, this quilt could pack a dramatic punch, or stay subtle and soft.

| Orange |
| Yellow-Orange |
| Yellow |

Question 60:
What is a split-complementary color scheme?

A split-complementary color scheme uses an analogous color scheme of any size variation and throws in the complementary color from the other side of the color wheel. This is a common arrangement in nature with

flowers providing excellent examples. Think about fuchsias, with their rich, red-pink colored petals, and how they are set off against the green of their leaves and stems. This is a classic split-complementary color scheme.

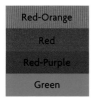

| Red-Orange |
| Red |
| Red-Purple |
| Green |

Question 61:
What is a triadic color scheme?

A triadic color scheme uses three colors equally spaced along the color wheel, like red, yellow, and blue or purple, orange, and green.

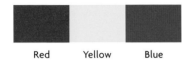

Red   Yellow   Blue

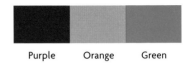

Purple   Orange   Green

Question 62:
Where can I find color inspiration?

This is a fun question as there is inspiration all around.

Your first stop should be right outside your front door. Nature provides you with limitless color possibilities. From the vibrant hues of flowers against the steady greens of their leaves to the changing tints of the sky during dawn and dusk, it is never possible to tire of the changing colorscapes around us. Take lots of photographs of the world around you. Make sure to look at the smallest beetle and the widest landscape for your inspiration files.

Another mandatory stop for inspiration is the museum or an art gallery. Look at the works of artists who came before you. How did they use color in their work? What unusual combinations did they devise and what was the effect on the piece?

Fashion offers yet another look into the world of color. Designers are always trying to offer new ways to work with color so that people will buy their clothes. Colors are worked into collections that try to maintain a consistent use of color. Many designers now have websites that post their entire current collections.

The photographs at the right show how picking key colors from the photographs can create a color scheme for your quilt.

ABOVE These beautiful blooms offer
a romantic color scheme.
By Jake Finch

ABOVE Look at how the white plays
with the bright red and pink.
By Jake Finch

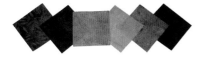

ABOVE Orange roses reflect subtle
changes of value, creating a wonderful
monochromatic color scheme.
By Jake Finch

ABOVE Can nature ever go wrong with
color? The striking parrots offer a great
starting point for a vibrant quilt.
By Jake Finch

FABRIC

Question 63:
What do I need to know about fabric?

Fabric is to quilters what paints are to painters and bronze is to sculptors. Fabric is the tool through which your art is accomplished. Most quilts are made from high-quality woven cotton fabrics, but there are plenty of quilts made from wool, silk, flannel, and other fibers and the quilter should not feel restricted to cotton.

Cotton is the best choice for most traditional quiltmaking because you will find the widest selection of color and pattern among cotton quilt-fabric companies. Also, cotton is the easiest fabric to bend to your will. Cotton's seams are crisp, its edges turn under beautifully for appliqué work, and different folding and manipulating techniques are carried out perfectly when it is used.

The quilt's results are easier to control when all of the fabrics are the same weight, but this can sometimes be achieved by using stabilizers with different fabrics, also.

Question 64:
What do I need to know about how fabric is designed and marketed?

Quilt fabrics work much the same way that clothing collections do. Seasonal fabric collections are released at regular intervals by fabric manufacturers; these feature a known designer or novelty theme. These fabrics are usually printed in one or two runs and when they are gone, they are gone. That's why if you see a fabric you've fallen in love with, you should purchase a little more than you think you need while it's in front of you.

Many manufacturers offer a core collection of their classics and blender lines. A blender is a fabric that usually reads like a solid, but might have some kind of texture or print to it. These fabrics are wonderful for "bridging" other fabrics in your stash. These are the workhorses of quilt fabrics and you can never have too many of them. Most designers will add a blender or two in their seasonal lines, but some fabric houses put out ongoing lines of different blenders.

Question 65:
Can I use something other than cotton in my quilts?

Absolutely! There are quilts made from all sorts of fabrics. Wool appliqué quilts are a traditional American art form and Victorian Crazy Quilts (see Question 10) incorporate every imaginable fine fabric available today.

Silks make beautiful additions to every kind of quilt. Be warned, though, that many silks need to be stabilized before using or they will shred in your quilt. There are many fusible stabilizers and interfacings on the market that can be used to reinforce silks and other delicate fabrics.

Question 66:
How do I prepare my fabric for making a quilt?

To prewash your fabrics or not to prewash your fabrics is one of the key debates in modern quilting.

Assuming you are working with cotton, I will weigh in on the issue by saying that yes, you should always prewash your fabrics. There are several reasons for this. They include:

• Most fabrics are finished with chemicals to make them easier to handle. Some people are allergic to these chemicals; washing will remove all traces of chemicals;

• Cotton shrinks and fabric from different manufacturers can shrink at different percentages. Prewashing your fabrics will also preshrink them so when you wash your quilt for the first time, you know that there will not be different shrinkage among different parts of your quilt;

• You can prep your fabrics for cutting when you take them from the dryer and iron them. This can be especially helpful if you're working with a directional print or a slightly off-grain weave; and

• Most important, some dyes are more prone to running. Prewashing will eliminate the possibility of having a dye run over your finished quilt. While it's true that most modern quilt fabric manufacturers have pretty much succeeded at preventing running dyes, there are exceptions and the last thing you want to have happen is to have your beautiful, time-intensive quilt ruined in the first wash because of a loose dye.

EXPERT TIP

❝ I prewash my cotton fabrics as soon as I get home from the store with them. I use a mild detergent (to prevent fading), cold water, and I iron the fabric when it comes out of the dryer, slightly damp. That way it's ready to go when I'm ready to use it. ❞

Question 67:
What are grain and bias?

The fabric's grain refers to the horizontal and vertical directions of the threads in the fabric's weave. When the fabric is folded or cut along the grain, the grain becomes the straight-line guide. When fabric is said to be "straight of grain" its grain line runs lengthwise; cross grain runs parallel to the fabric's width. Some quilt shops will tear fabric (instead of cutting) along the grain when you buy from them. If they do, buy a little extra so you can straighten the torn edges.

A fabric cut on the bias means the fabric is cut along the grain's diagonal, at a 45-degree angle, which creates a cut edge that is very unstable and stretchy. A bias cut provides more flexibility when the fabric needs to be sewn or folded along a grain. So, many quilters will cut their binding strips along the bias when they want to maneuver binding along a serpentine (curved/waved) border. Bias-cut strips are also handy in appliqué when you might need vine strips or other pieces that have a little more give to them.

When you are cutting pieces for most straight-edged patchwork, you'll want to stay along the grain to prevent the pieces from fraying and to ensure accurate measurements.

Question 68:
How do I choose fabrics for my design?

This should be the fun part for most quilters—choosing the fabrics. There are two main things to consider when selecting your fabrics: color and visual texture.

Let's assume you're working with cotton fabrics for this project. You can go with the tried-and-true method of working from a focus fabric, which is generally a print containing several or many colors. If you're using a paisley print, for instance, look at the main, background color found in the fabric. That would be your primary color. Then, look at the other colors

ABOVE With its large scale and many colors, there's no doubt that this beautiful Asian print can stand out as your quilt's focus fabric. Use the colors and textures within this print to choose the secondary fabrics.

ABOVE With its all-over pattern and subtle color changes, this fabric serves as a unique blender fabric. Blenders give your eyes a "rest" as they travel over the quilt's design. Most designs benefit from having rest spots.

ABOVE This feathered clamshell print provides additional texture in the fabric choices. It is also a directional print and needs to be handled with deliberation.

ABOVE Even though this fabric has a lot going on visually—a Geisha scenic print similar to a toile print—it will work well as a secondary fabric for the focus fabric because its monochromatic color scheme doesn't compete for attention.

ABOVE This bamboo print runs vertically and offers the feel of stripes. This can be an effective print, offering "movement" within the quilt's design. As with any directional print, you'll want to be careful to cut the fabric to best enhance the directional print, and position the fabric deliberately.

ABOVE A small, busy print using the same colors as the focus fabric can play a strong supporting role in your quilt's design, for example in the border. With a similar theme of Asian cranes, it's a fun choice that commands a little more attention.

used in the print. All of these can provide a palette for your other color choices. You also want to look at the percentage of color used in the print. If you only have a small bit of yellow in the print, then yellow can become your accent color. Since the fabric designer has already done the work of balancing out the colors in the fabric, use what's already there when making your choices.

Texture comes from the type of prints used, their effect on the quilt as a whole, and on the individual parts of the quilt.

A tiny polka dot will offer one

texture, one that is generally easy on the eyes, where a wild floral will often dominate a design. There are no hard rules about the different prints you use in designing a quilt, but you do want there to be a balance.

You also need to consider how much of a fabric will be shown in the piece it's used within. Picture using a big bright novelty print featuring a fire truck for a boy's quilt. You know you will only use two inches of it for a simple block within the quilt. That means you will probably only see a small slice of that truck in the quilt and the fabric's effect will be lost.

If you're unsure about the colors and textures you're trying out in the quilt, use your sketchbook and crayons to sketch it out with the colors and make a sample block with the fabrics. Try it out. The worst that will happen is you will make a different choice.

Question 69:
What is visual texture and how can I use it?

With fabric, texture comes from the print of the fabric. Most quilter's cottons will not have an apparent texture in the weave. But you can create great visual interest with the limitless variety of printed fabrics.

Small prints with only subtle color changes will "read" more like a solid fabric. Large busy prints will stand by themselves. Prints with several colors will be busy. Muted shades in printed fabrics will tend to blend into the other fabrics in a quilt's choices.

To achieve a good balance of textures from your fabrics, choose a variety of prints in different scales and try not to repeat them, unless that's the effect you're going for. For instance, if you have a small polka dot with a large focus floral and a multicolored stripe all in the same block, you've got a lot of interest going on. If the colors work together, this will be a stunning block.

But you may also be collecting a type of fabric, like plaids, to feature in a quilt. Just using a collection of similar fabrics (stripes, flowers, themed, plaids) makes the quilt seem more fun.

Try out your fabrics before you commit to them. Whether you're shopping at a store or shopping in your stash, lay out your selections, one on top of the other and see how the fabrics work together. Just like with composition, balance, and color, you will begin to train your eye to recognize what works best.

ABOVE Selecting fabrics from the same designer collection is one way to safely work with visual texture because your colors will all match. But it also serves as a good example of how the same color scheme can be worked in different fabric choices to provide lots of different textures. Fabrics are *Roman Holiday* by 3 Sisters for Moda.

Question 70:
What is selvage?

The selvage is the long, finished edge of the fabric. It spans the length of the fabric. Most fabric companies will use the selvage to print the name and designer of the fabric, and you might also have a series of colored dots showing on the selvage. These are the colors found in the fabric's print and this can be very helpful for matching fabrics.

Try to keep the info from the selvage until your project is completed. If you run out of fabric in the middle of a project, this information can help you track down some additional fabric.

Most quilting cotton fabrics are milled on looms that create fabric that is 44 inches wide. To accommodate variances and shrinkage, assume a 40-inch fabric width.

Question 71:
How much fabric should I buy if I don't have a project in mind?

A big part of this decision comes down to budget. Assuming that you have some money to spend on expanding your stash, the smallest cut of fabric you want to invest in is a half yard. Quarter yard cuts, at 9 inches by 44 inches, are just too limiting. Most patterns will have something to use a half yard for. If you really love the fabric, consider buying a yard or two or three. If the fabric's print is large, having at least a yard will also help for designing.

If your design calls for fussy cutting—isolating a design element to use as an appliqué piece or to center in a patch or block—buy extra yardage.

Question 72:
How do I know how big a cut of fabric will be?

Yards	Inches (length x width)
1/8 yard	4 1/2" x 40"
1/4 yard	9" x 40"
1/3 yard	12" x 40"
1/2 yard	16" x 40"
2/3 yard	24" x 40"
7/8 yard	31 1/2" x 40"
1 yard	36" x 40"

Question 73:
What are all of those specialty cuts out there?

In recent years, the quilt industry has answered the quilter's call for getting the most types of fabric and quilt projects from the simplest groupings. That's where the specialty cuts come in. From 2 1/2-inch strips to triangles and charm squares, pre-packaged fabric collections all cut in the same size and shape provide an easy purchase for fabric hounds.

Even better news is that quilt designers are constantly working with these specialty cuts to offer quilt projects made just from these fabrics, with maybe the simple addition of a yard or two of supporting fabrics. From books to patterns, there's a way to make a quilt from these cut collections without any pain and with far less time.

Question 74:
What is a fat quarter?

A very popular specialty cut, a fat quarter is 18 inches by 22 inches. A standard quarter yard of quilt fabric would be 9 inches by 44 inches, which is a very awkward size to use in quiltmaking.

A fat quarter, which has the same area of fabric, provides a much more useful shape, takes a half-yard of fabric (18 inches by 44 inches) and cuts it in half along the width. So, a half-yard of fabric will yield two fat quarters. Patterns and books featuring fat quarter patterns are plentiful. Quilt shops regularly carry fat quarters and many coordinate them in bundles for ease in designing a quilt. A good quilt shop will also cut a fat quarter from a bolt when asked. Fat quarters are also good for use in small craft projects. Bundled together they make a great gift for a quilter.

Question 75:
What is a fat eighth?

A fat eighth is a cut of fabric measuring 9 inches by 22 inches. These are handy cuts for novelty quilts and scrap quilts, though not as flexible in use as the fat quarter.

EXPERT TIP

66 If you have a favorite cut of fabric you turn to most when working on a quilt, consider cutting that piece when you buy a new fabric. You can make your favorite cuts (fat quarters, 2 ½-inch strips) ready for a project at a moment's notice. 99

Question 76:
What is a strip roll or other types of common strip cuts?

Strip rolls are 2 ½-inch strip collections. At 2 ½ inches, a strip of fabric can be sewn to other strips and they become extremely versatile. Entire fabric collections can be gathered together, usually somewhere around 30 to 40 strips, and this becomes a jelly roll.

Other strips gathered into rolls include 6-inch strips. Again, by cutting and sewing these strips together, the quilter can achieve many different types of quilt designs.

RIGHT Jelly Rolls by Moda Fabrics are pre-cut fabric collections that are very popular with today's quilters. Because they are pre-cut, there's time saved in the quilt project's construction. Quilt designers are answering the call by providing lots of patterns designed to work with pre-cut fabrics.

Question 77:
What size is a charm square?

Charm squares are generally 5- or 6-inch square pieces of quilt fabric. Charm squares are a great way to get a lot of variety in a quilt without a huge investment of money. Many fabric companies package new collections in charm squares, making these packs very collectible cuts of fabric for quilters.

Question 78:
What about shopping for fabric online?

Shopping for fabrics online is a wonderful alternative to having a shop near you, but you need to be careful about your perception of color from your computer screen.

If you already know the fabric or the design line, then ordering your fabric through an online retailer makes sense. There are many retailers available online and some offer wish lists and design boards on their sites, which will assist in the design process.

But, if you're looking to fill in a fabric selection for a quilt and you're looking at fabrics fresh online, your colors can be so off as to render the fabric unusable when it arrives in the mail. Some retailers may offer a swatch, but even if you're matching a fabric that you already have a sample for, note that dye lots will affect the fabric's coloration.

I use online sources when I'm shopping a collection I know and when I'm having fun and something catches my eye. I almost never try to match a fabric online.

Question 79:
When I run out of a fabric, how can I track down more of the same?

This is where keeping the selvage is helpful. By knowing the manufacturer and the collection and the designer, you have a better chance of locating that fabric.

First visit your local shop, or better yet, the shop where you purchased the fabric. They may have some more lingering around, or be able to re-order some for you.

If that doesn't work, call the manufacturer and ask if they've sold that same fabric to anyone else in the area, or someone who runs an Internet quilt shop. If they can't tell you, you can always start calling other shops in your area.

If you belong to a guild, you can also bring a sample to your meeting, ask if anyone else has that fabric, and offer to buy it. Your local shop owner might also be willing to have you post a snip of the fabric and a note on a bulletin board at the shop.

Scouring eBay can also uncover hard-to-find fabrics. I've been able to get some missing fabrics from online auction sellers several times just by searching the manufacturer and the collection's name.

Finally, and this is my favorite source, there's a website (isn't there always?) called www.missingfabrics. com that serves as an online bulletin board for missing quilt fabrics.

7
CUTTING

Question 80:
How do I use a rotary cutter?

A rotary cutter is a marvelous quilting tool, but it's also extremely dangerous. Rotary safety should always be your first priority when working on a project because the potential to hurt yourself or someone else is so high.

BELOW The invention of the rotary cutter literally changed the face of quilting. With its exact cuts and accompanying rulers and mats, quilters could toss their cardboard templates away forever.

I strongly recommend that you purchase a rotary cutter that has a safety mechanism. Certain brands have a rotary cutter that retracts when your hand releases the grip. It's too easy to lay a cutter on a table with the blade exposed. With the retraction mechanism, the blade will be covered again.

If you are working with a standard rotary cutter in which you are responsible for always closing the blade, make this a habit right from the start of your quilting career. It's

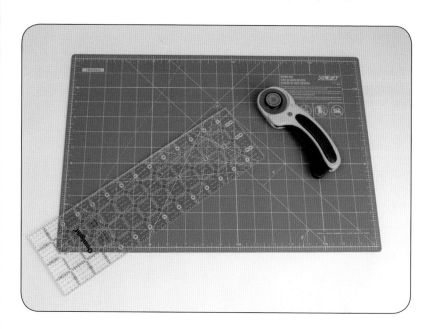

an easy enough motion to close the blade after each and every cut.

Make sure your rotary cutter is kept away from children while you're working and when you're done. This is a cool-looking tool and children seem to be drawn to the rotary cutter as if it's candy.

Change your blades regularly.

A dull blade will make you push and work harder, which lessens your control with the blade. If there are any nicks in the blade, this will create gaps in your cutting.

Wear closed-toe shoes when using a rotary cutter. A dropped open blade can do real damage.

Question 81:
How do I change my blade?

Most blades have a nut that will be unscrewed on the opposite side of the cutter from the blade. There is usually a washer that holds the blade in place as well. Place the rotary cutter on a stable surface, blade side down. Unscrew the nut and remove the washer and place them next to you in the order you've removed them. Carefully turn the cutter over to the blade side and lay on the surface for support. There is a cover on the blade that will lift off. Your blade is now loose. Very carefully, slide the blade off of the cutter's handle, making sure you are not holding your hand in such a way as to close inadvertently over the exposed

blade. Again, safety is the most important concern. The old blade will need to be carefully disposed of by putting it into a closed, solid container. Take the new blade from its case, place it on the cutter's handle and secure it with the blade cover. Again, carefully turn the cutter over (The blade can slip—watch it!) and replace the washer and then the nut, tightening the nut until it's secure. Your blade is ready to use. I store my old machine needles and rotary blades in a small coffee tin with a plastic lid that has a hole in it. I drop the needles into the lid and open it to carefully place the blades. When it's full, it gets tossed safely into the trash.

1 Rotary cutter and extra blades.

2 Turn the rotary cutter to the side without the blade.

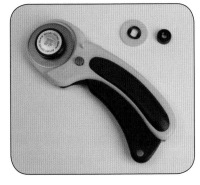

3 Remove the nut and the washer and place in order on your work surface.

4 Carefully turn the rotary cutter back to the blade side.

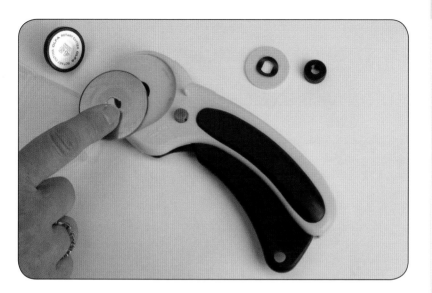

5 Remove the blade's cover and carefully slide the used blade off of the cutter and into a solid container. Place the new blade on the cutter's handle and follow with the blade's cover. Carefully turn the cutter over and put the washer and nut back onto the cutter, tightening it well. It's ready to use.

Question 82:
I'm left-handed. How can my cutter work for me?

Some rotary cutters are designed to work for either lefties or righties. If you're right-handed, the blade is installed on the left side of the cutter, so it will butt up against the right edge of your rotary ruler.

If you're left-handed, you can install the blade on the right side of the rotary cutter and butt the blade against the left edge of the rotary ruler. Simply switch the blade's side and make sure you maintain the order of the washer, blade, and nut.

Question 83:
How do I safely hold a rotary cutter while cutting?

When you're holding the handle of the rotary cutter, make sure your entire hand is wrapped around it. Do not place a finger along the top to guide your hand. It's too easy to have your hand slip and run over the top of the blade while you're cutting.

Always, always use a self-healing rotary cutting mat for your cutting tasks. This mat provides a grid with which to work and the mat's material also grips the blade as it cuts, offering additional safety measures. Using anything else runs the risk of losing control of the blade, or dulling its edge.

Never, never drag the rotary cutter toward you when cutting fabric. Always work away from your body. If you're cutting in an area where someone can stand or walk past the other side of the surface, make sure they're not there when you cut. Again, it's too easy to slip and cut them if they are standing in front of you.

You don't want to saw through your fabric. Your cutting should be done in one smooth, continuous fashion.

Start with your fabric neatly pressed and folded, if necessary. Line up the folded edge of your fabric along one of the cutting mat's grid lines. With your ruler placed on top of the fabric, start from the fabric end closest to you and push the blade away from you in one continuous motion. If the piece of fabric is long, you might have to stop halfway through the cut, realign the ruler, and continue. Make sure the fabric is always on the mat. Also, you want to apply steady and firm pressure to the rotary cutter. You need to be in control of the cutter at all times.

Learning the proper use of the rotary cutter is an important time-saver for your quilting. With practice, this tool will become one of your favorites, as long as you always respect its power.

Question 84:
How do I best cut with a rotary cutter mat?

Holding the ruler correctly is the key to successful cutting. When you're first stocking your tool case with rotary supplies, you can make do for most cutting with a 6 by 24-inch ruler or an 8 ½ by 24-inch ruler. These sizes allow the most flexibility in your cuts. From there, invest in a 12-inch or 15-inch square ruler and possibly a 4- by 14-inch ruler. These are not essential, but will help in your cutting tasks.

The most common problem with rotary cutting is that the ruler can slip while you're cutting, creating a bad cut in your fabric. There are several tools on the market to help prevent this. One is sandpaper dots that adhere to the back of the ruler and grip the fabric as you cut. If you can't find the dots, you can make your own with double-stick tape and small scraps of medium-grade sandpaper.

There are also handles that help to disburse your hand's pressure more accurately on the ruler. These usually have suction cups and some kind of grip.

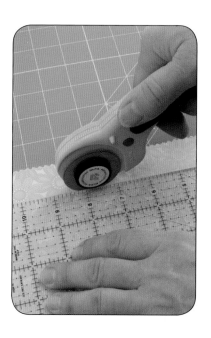

ABOVE With your ruler placed on top of the fabric, start from the fabric end closest to you and push the blade away from you in one continuous motion.

HOW IT'S DONE

With practice, you should be able to accomplish most cutting without the extra tools.

- Working with a long ruler, position your left hand to the left side of the ruler (assuming you're a rightie—if you're left-handed, switch sides through these instructions), and drop your pinkie over the ruler's edge to anchor the ruler down. Then, making sure your fingers are nowhere near the ruler's right edge, start cutting the fabric from the bottom to the top of the ruler.
- Make sure that your rotary cutter's blade edge is right up against the ruler's edge.
- You can angle the rotary blade just slightly away from the ruler's edge and this will give you a clean cut.

EXPERT TIP

I use a 60 mm rotary blade for most of my cutting because it can easily cut through six to eight layers of fabric at once, and I'm a lazy quilter. This only works with very sharp blades and you have to be careful to keep the pressure even and not allow the fabrics to shift under the blade and ruler. However, it can be a great time-saver, even to cut four layers at one time.

Question 85:
What about templates? Can I use them instead?

In the not-so-olden days of quilting, cardboard templates and scissors were used to cut the quilt's fabrics. Templates are also used in appliqué. So, yes, you absolutely can use templates.

Several different types of template plastic can be found in the market, which will create the cleanest line for cutting fabric. Some template plastic is designed to withstand the heat of an iron and this is best saved for appliqué. Cardboard is still an option, but if you're cutting lots of shapes with a cardboard template, the cardboard will wear down quickly. With template plastic, you can use it over and over without worrying about the edges wearing down.

Simply trace the template shape (usually found in the quilt's pattern) onto the template plastic with a permanent, extra-fine line marker. Carefully cut the shape from the plastic making sure its straight lines are steady and nick-free. Then, with some kind of marking pen or pencil which can be removed later, trace the shape onto your fabric and cut with a rotary cutter and mat, or with scissors, adding seam allowance as directed by the pattern. Templates can be very handy for traveling projects.

8

MACHINE PIECING

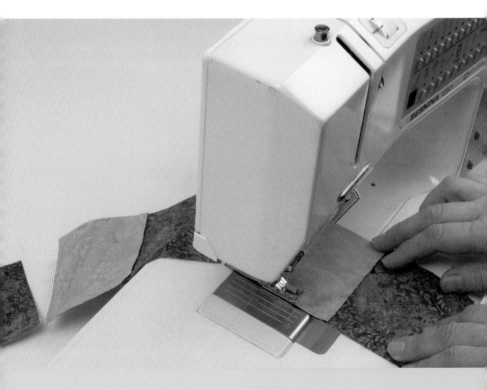

Question 86:
What kind of thread do I use?

For most machine piecing, a high-quality cotton thread will serve your needs perfectly. Gutterman, J.P. Coats, Mettler, Superior, YLI, and Aurifil are just several of the many brands available. Many quilters use only cotton threads because most quilts are made solely from cotton. I have even heard that using polyester blend threads is harmful to cotton quilts because the synthetic material is stronger than cotton and over time it will wear through your quilt. I'm not sure if I completely believe this, but it probably won't do any harm to stick with cotton for your piecing.

For most of your projects, you will probably only need a small selection of neutral colored threads. Gray (medium and dark), tan, ivory, and red will carry you through almost all of your projects. The thread will blend into the fabrics as long as there isn't much contrast between the colors.

Make sure your thread isn't old. You don't want the thread to break as it works through your machine, and old thread will often suffer a breakdown of the fibers. If your thread does start breaking, toss it and buy new thread.

I prefer a fine to extra-fine thread, 40-to-60 weight. With threads, the larger the number, the finer the thread. Long-staple Egyptian cotton is always nice. The longer the staple, the less fraying will occur.

Question 87:
What about my machine needles?

Sewing machine needles come in many sizes and shapes and the needles can literally make or break your sewing.

Most standard cotton thread will be best served by a sharps needle in a 70/10, 80/12 or 90/14 size. A sharps needle has a sharp point to the needle. The first number in the size is the European listing and the second number is the American listing. The smaller the numbers, the smaller the needles. All mainstream needles list both numbers on them.

For the thinner weight threads (50 or 60 weight) use the 70/10 needle if you can find it. If not, the 80/12 will work.

Machine quilting and specialty threads will use different needles and some of those specifics are covered in the chapter on machine quilting. But for basic piecing, a sharps needle will suit you fine.

Quilters and sewers are notorious for not changing their machine needles often enough. Machine needles will dull and when they start dulling, your stitching and thread will suffer. I change my needles at the start of every project, and if I'm doing some heavy-duty sewing through many layers I'll change the needle for every couple of bobbin changes. If you listen to your machine working, you'll be able to tell when your needle is pushing too hard through the fabric. It will start sounding like it's pounding through your work.

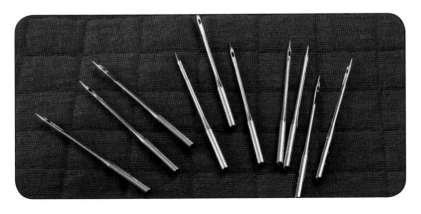

Question 88:
What about the bobbin?

When it comes to basic piecing, I use the same thread in the top and the bobbin, and, I prefer finer, high-quality cotton threads. For machine quilting, I use threads made specifically for the bobbin, but that's covered in Question 156.

Prepare at least two bobbins before you start your stitching to make sure you don't get frustrated when you run out.

Over time, your bobbins can wear out. This applies mostly to plastic bobbins. If you find your thread is breaking or your machine is jamming, you might need to toss the bobbin. There could be a microscopic nick in the plastic that snags on the thread. Bobbins are easy to replace through the manufacturer or at a fabric store's notions rack. Your machine might even use a universal bobbin and it's simple to stock up on these.

Wind your bobbin following the sewing machine guide's directions. Having the proper tension during the winding is important. If there's any problem during the winding, such as the thread becomes loose or wound around the stick that holds the bobbin, remove all of the

thread from the bobbin and start over. Loose bobbin thread can jam the bobbin casing and create a huge mess in your machine.

The bobbin casing also has a tension setting. Sometimes, the casing is removable. Other times, it rests permanently in the machine. Some types of specialty thread might require a tension adjustment to the bobbin casing for greater success. You'll need to refer to your sewing machine manual for this information and make sure to make any adjustments to the casing slowly and slightly. It's too easy to over-adjust tension on a sewing machine.

Question 89:
What's tension?

Tension is the pull on the thread as it passes through the sewing machine or bobbin. Most sewing machines have a tension dial on the front of the machine with numbers ranging from zero to nine. Most of your standard sewing on a machine in good working order will use a tension between 3.5 and 6.

When your tension is off, you will know because the threads will either look like they're falling off of the fabric or they will pull so tightly in the fabric that the seam puckers. Try adjusting the tension dial with very small adjustments. It shouldn't take much to see an improvement in the stitching.

If your tension never seems to improve enough, consider taking your machine to the dealer or a reputable repairman. Sewing machines, like most complex machinery, need to be tuned up regularly and if your machine has not been serviced in at least a year, that could be the problem.

If you are machine quilting, sewing through very thick or very thin projects, or have specialty threads in your machine, you will probably have to adjust the tension to allow for these differences. Again, make slight adjustments each time and when you find the perfect combination of project/material to tension, write it down somewhere you will be able to locate easily.

Question 90:
Do I have to pin my pieces?

Usually, you do. Don't be afraid of pins. They are there to help you, not hurt you. But, like everything else in quilting, there's a better way to do it.

First, use pins that are appropriate to the task. I mostly work with extra-long, glass-head pins (about 1 1/2-inch long). I use pins by Clover and while these pins are a little pricier than others, I prefer them because they are super thin and move easily through fabric.

You should stock your sewing case with long pins, silk pins (usually short and very fine), appliqué pins (which are even shorter), and large safety pins for basting and grouping pieces. A pin cushion is also helpful.

When you're pinning fabric pieces before sewing them together, you want to line up the edges exactly and put your pin in perpendicular to the edge. In other words, create a right angle with your pin in your fabric. If you're pinning large pieces of fabric together, such as a border to a quilt top, plan on pinning every 3 inches.

When you're sewing your pinned pieces together, DO NOT sew over the pins! If your machine's needle hits the pin in just the wrong way,

you can break the pin and/or the needle, jam the machine, and possibly have small pieces of metal flying. Sew along the seam, stop just before the pin starts traveling under the foot, and remove the pin to place it in a pin cushion.

From my list of safety measures comes these thoughts: Please don't hold pins in your mouth. Our mothers were crazy to do this. It's too easy to have them drop onto the floor and I suppose you could swallow one or stab your face if you weren't careful. Also, if you think you've lost a pin or a needle, stop what you're doing to find it! Pins and needles create big problems in the bodies of humans and animals alike.

Question 91:
How do I ensure an accurate ¼-inch seam?

Almost nothing is more important in quilting than an accurate ¼-inch seam. When you piece a traditional patchwork block, it's the ¼-inch seam that keeps the block's size true throughout the construction.

Let's say that you're off by ¹⁄₁₆-inch on your seam allowance. By the time you sew all of your block's

components together, you can find your measurements are off by inches and the blocks can't be joined together because they are all different sizes.

Luckily for us quilters there are several ways to make sure that you are getting a ¼-inch seam allowance. First, purchase a ¼-inch foot for your sewing machine. Almost every sewing machine manufacturer on the market will have a ¼-inch foot for their machines. There are also generic ¼-inch feet available through large notions retailers, like *Nancy's Notions* and *Clotilde*. Of course, you'll need to find out if the generic version will fit your machine, and this is usually determined by whether the shank (the arm holding the machine's feet) is long or short.

Bernina machines have a completely different shank style and you may need an adapter.

Some ¼-inch feet have a lip on the right edge of the foot that follows along the fabric's edge. These are just a little more helpful to use for sewing, so it's worth the purchase if your machine can use one.

HOW IT'S DONE

- If you haven't found a ¼-inch foot or you just want some extra help in making sure you're at a ¼-inch seam allowance, take a piece of paper with a straight edge and draw a line from top to bottom along the right hand edge at exactly a ¼-inch. (A rotary ruler should be used for this as it's the easiest way to measure.)
- Place the paper under your sewing machine needle, lowering the needle on the right edge of the drawn line.
- Then, without any thread in the machine, sew along the line until you're halfway down the paper.
- Stop sewing and make sure your needle is down in the paper.
- Take some masking tape and carefully place the tape on the machine's bed, along the right edge of the paper.
- Make sure the tape sits from the front of the machine's bed to the back.
- When you remove the paper, the tape is now placed at a ¼-inch.

To test your ¼-inch seams for accuracy, piece a nine-patch block. Accurately cut nine squares at 3 ½ inches each from fabric, piece them together using a ¼-inch seam and press. Then, measure the finished block. Your block should be 9 ½ inches square. If it's not, either your piecing is off or your ¼-inch guide (no matter what you're using) is off.

Question 92:
How do I piece a block?

Most quilt patterns and books will have instructions on how to piece a block. For simple patchwork involving squares, triangles, and rectangles, you'll have two pieces of fabric, right sides together, lined up along the pieces' straight edges. Place the unit under your sewing machine foot and, following your ¼-inch marking or foot, stitch from the unit's top to the bottom. If you use a smaller stitch length, around 1.8 or 2 on most machines, you'll probably not need to back-stitch your first couple of stitches. Back-stitching is when you start stitching about a ½-inch below the unit's top with a reverse stitch, get to the top edge of the unit, and then start stitching the unit in the forward stitch. A back stitch provides extra security from the unit's seam splitting during pressing and handling, but a shorter stitch length should accomplish the same task.

Question 93:
What does it mean to nestle my seams?

When two seams pressed in opposite directions are sewn together accurately, one seam will sit to the right and one to the left, creating a perfect cross where the four pieces of fabric come together. This cross allows the flattest possible joining of the seams and it's called nestling. Whenever you join seams together, you should strive for perfect nestling. This will create perfect intersections from the quilt's front. Using pins will help achieve this.

ABOVE When your seams are properly nestled, they will meet exactly at the intersection of the four seams. Nestled seams feel level when you hold them in your hands.

Question 94:
How do I press my seams?

Pressing seams is an art of its own and, while not difficult, there are some tips to do it well. Unlike clothing construction where you usually press a seam open, in quilting you'll press most seams to one side of the pieced fabric. Usually you'll press the seam to the darker fabric so the seam doesn't show through to a light colored fabric piece. But, if you're following a quilt pattern, do defer to the pattern's pressing instructions if there are any. Sometimes more accurate piecing of the block is accomplished by specific pressing directions.

When you press your seams, gently open the fabric piece, right-side down on the ironing surface. Pick the direction in which you'll be pressing the seam down and with the long side of the iron, smooth the seam in that direction. Start moving the iron not on the seam but on the fabric area next to it. Make sure there are no creases on the right side of the fabric piece.

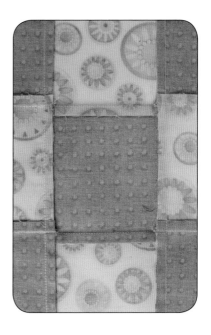

ABOVE Most good quilt patterns will provide pressing instructions for the quilt, which will help the seams to nestle and match as well as possible.

EXPERT TIP

❝ If there is a crease, re-press from the wrong side again, not the right side. You don't want to put seam line impressions on the front of the quilt. ❞

Question 95:
What is chain piecing?

Chain piecing is one of the many wonderful ways modern quilters speed up their projects. Strip piecing lends itself beautifully to assembly-line-style quiltmaking. Since you don't need to raise and lower your presser feet repetitively, or stop and snip threads until the end, you're able to save lots of time in your quilt's construction.

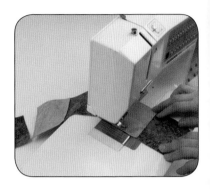

When working with repetitive or similar units, stack the units neatly, line them up near your machine bed, and feed them one after the other under your machine's feet. This creates a string of sewn units that just need to be snipped apart and pressed.

ABOVE By lining up your fabric pairs and feeding them one after the other under the machine's needle, you will be able to piece your quilt much faster.

Question 96:
What are dog ears?

Sometimes, after you've pieced a unit and pressed its seam open, you see a small piece of the seam sticking out from the unit's shape. This is called a dog ear and happens mostly with triangles and other unusual shapes. Just trim the seam to match the unit's intended shape and move on to the next step.

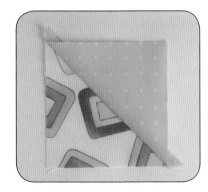

9
TRIANGLES

Question 97:
What is a half-square triangle?

A sewn square that is bisected by a diagonal line creating two equal triangles is called a half-square triangle.

Half-square triangles can be the bane of a quilter's life because it's too easy for shifting to occur when piecing them, especially if the triangles are small. Also, because the long edge is usually cut along the bias, it can stretch during sewing.

Fortunately, there are many, many resources and tools on the market, from rulers to papers, all designed to take the pain out of sewing half-square triangles.

The reason that so many resources exist in the quilt industry to conquer the half-square triangle is because this simple geometric concoction serves as the root for many different quilt blocks and patterns.

BELOW Half-square triangle.

Question 98:
What is the math to figure out the size of triangles from squares?

To create triangles suitable for piecing together to become half-square triangles, you can cut a square in half diagonally once (making two triangles) or twice (making four triangles).

To calculate the original size of the square needed to get two triangles that, when sewn together with a $\frac{1}{4}$-inch seam allowance, becomes a half-square triangle, add $\frac{7}{8}$-inch to the finished measurement. So, if you want a 1-inch finished square made up of two half-square triangles, you'll cut the triangles from a 1 $\frac{7}{8}$-inch square.

To calculate the original size of the square needed to get four triangles that, when two are sewn together with a $\frac{1}{4}$-inch seam allowance, becomes a half-square triangle, add 1 $\frac{1}{4}$-inches to the finished measurement. So, if you want a 1-inch finished square made up of two half-square triangles, you'll cut the four triangles from a 2 $\frac{1}{4}$-inch square.

When you cut the triangles from the squares, make sure you maintain the grainline along the straight edges of the pre-cut squares.

Question 99:
How do I piece half-square triangles?

If you're not using one of the many paper piecing patterns to make the job of creating half-square triangles easier, then place the two triangles, right sides together, and sew a $\frac{1}{4}$-inch seam along the long edge.

Try not to stretch the triangles, which is easy to do along the long bias edge. Press the seam allowance to the darker fabric.

10
PAPER PIECING

Question 100:
What is paper piecing?

Paper piecing, sometimes called foundation piecing, uses a paper pattern as a sewing guide for your quilt block or unit. You actually sew the fabric to the paper pattern. The paper is removed at a later point.

Paper piecing is best used for blocks requiring very sharp points, straight lines, and/or intricate piecework. Accomplished paper piecers can break down any image into tiny, straight-edged components to create complex pictures within their quilts. Paper piecing can also save time as the measuring is taken out of the design since the pattern is drawn on the paper.

Question 101:
Why would I use paper piecing to make a block?

Since paper piecing ensures accurate piecing of otherwise challenging points and segments, it makes sense to use it for any complex quilt.

RIGHT *Mrs. Froggy's Dowry*, made by Jake Finch from a design by Peggy Martin from her book, *Quick Strip Paper Piecing* (C&T Publishing) uses paper piecing to create the star.

Question 102:
How do I work with paper piecing patterns?

Many well-known paper piecing pattern designers provide the paper foundations with their patterns. (Judy Niemeyer at www.quiltworx. com immediately comes to mind.) Other patterns and most books will provide the pattern images and ask you to photocopy the patterns onto paper for home use.

Make sure if you're photocopying an assortment of patterns, whether all the same pattern or several different kinds, that you copy them all at one time on one machine. There is distortion between machines and you won't want to get partway through your quilt only to find that your blocks are not matching up. Also, make several extra copies in case you make a mistake in the piecing.

Your pattern or book should provide detailed directions on working with the patterns. Follow them. Most paper piecing patterns have numbers to indicate the order in which you'll sew the pieces together. There are also a couple of techniques used for the trimming of the pieces. Without adding confusion, I say defer to the directions and follow them very carefully. Most paper piecing techniques have you sewing a block or pattern in a reverse pattern and it can be confusing while you're doing the work. I always tell my students to suspend their inclination to think through the steps and just to do one step at a time. After a couple of blocks, the piecing begins to make sense.

EXPERT TIP

66 Because paper piecing is really sewing in reverse, it can be confusing, especially to a seasoned quilter. I have my students write out the steps for paper piecing (depends on the method you choose to follow) on a self-stick sheet and stick it on the front of their sewing machine so they can't forget what they're doing. 99

Question 103:
What kind of paper do I use?

Yet another great quilting debate can be fought over what kind of paper to use when copying your paper piecing patterns. I use plain copy paper because I have a copier at home and this is what's easiest for me to use. It's a little thicker than the market offers for paper piecers, but I've never had a problem with it.

Some paper piecers swear by velum or tissue paper. These alternatives are usually simpler to remove from your fabric when you're done with your piecing.

There are more than a handful of companies providing paper-piecing paper to the quilt marketplace. All of these are designed to work in printers and copiers.

There is even a type of paper that dissolves in water. Of course this creates an extra step in the project—soaking your blocks—but I've had a couple of students who use it.

Whatever you use, just be consistent and find what works best for your needs.

Question 104:
When do I remove the paper?

Start by adjusting your stitch length to be smaller. The smaller stitch length serves to perforate the paper, which will help remove it later. Don't remove the paper until the block or unit is joined to the next one. When it is time to remove the paper, fold the paper along the stitching line, which should have perforated the paper during the

sewing. Carefully tug the paper to start a tear at one end and continue to gently pull the paper from the fabric. You don't want to loosen the threads or separate the seam from too much pressure. If you have a piece of paper that won't tear easily, use a pin to carefully lift the paper from the fabric. Don't puncture your fabric if possible.

11
HAND PIECING

Question 105:
What do I need in my traveling tool kit for hand piecing?

Hand piecing is a wonderful way to take along a quilt project. Famed master quilter Jinny Beyer handpieces and handquilts her award-winning projects and many were done while she watched her kids participate in sports.

Putting together a small tool kit for your hand piecing is a snap and you probably already have most of the supplies on hand:

- Small scissors for snipping threads and fabric
- Scissors for cutting cardboard or template plastic
- Small or medium rotary cutter
- Small rotary ruler (1-inch by 12-inch size will work fine)
- Small rotary cutting mat
- Fine-point mechanical pencil
- White chalk pencil
- Template material
- Extra-fine permanent marker in black
- An assortment of hand needles in different sizes
- Pins
- Thread
- Seam ripper
- Lap table or clipboard
- Thimble
- Thread conditioner

Question 106:
How do I prepare my pattern pieces for hand piecing?

Because you won't be relying upon your ¼-inch sewingmachine foot or a marking on the sewingmachine bed to establish your ¼-inch seam allowance, you'll need to work with traditional templates and drawn lines instead before sewing your pieces together. This shouldn't take much time to accomplish and it's a completely portable process.

Start by making the template pieces for your block. Working with template plastic is the easiest and sturdiest way to go, but you can work with heavy cardboard if you prefer. Take a line drawing of the block you wish to create (lightly colored to represent which fabrics you'll be using,) and determine which pieces making up the block need to be created for templates. Not every piece will need its own template as most blocks use repetitive shapes for its construction. For each individual piece, assign a letter or number to the piece. Then, place the template plastic over the drawing and carefully copy each piece's outline to the plastic with the permanent marker. Use a ruler for straight edges and leave space between the pieces. Then cut each template piece out using sharp scissors.

If you're working with cardboard, trace the outlines onto tracing paper or freezer paper's dull side and then roughly cut the pieces out, glue or iron the pieces onto the cardboard, then carefully trim the pieces on the lines.

You now have your templates ready for tracing. Prepare your fabric by prewashing and ironing. Place the template, rightside down, on the fabric's wrong side, making sure to follow the fabric's grainlines. With your pencil (mechanical for most colored fabric, white chalk pencil for the darkest fabrics) carefully trace the outline of each template piece onto the fabric. Make sure there is at least a ¾-inch space between each marked piece.

With the rotary cutter, carefully cut out each piece using the ruler to add a ¼-inch seam allowance around each piece's outline. Your pieces are now ready to be assembled.

ABOVE With your pencil (mechanical for most colored fabric, white chalk pencil for the darkest fabrics) carefully trace the outline of each template piece onto the fabric.

ABOVE With the rotary cutter, carefully cut out each piece using the ruler to add a ¼-inch seam allowance around each piece's outline.

Question 107:
What about my needle and thread?

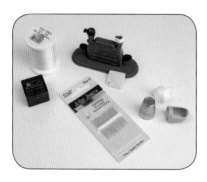

ABOVE Needle threader, thimbles, hand needles, and thread.

Needles in hand piecing are a very personal preference. Generally, you want to use needles that are thin and of good quality. Usually, the thinner the needle, the finer the stitch. Look at betweens, sharps, and milliner's needles. These are all thin needles. Betweens are shorter and are also used for hand quilting. Sharps are slightly longer, and milliner's are the longest. I find it difficult to hold the sharps and betweens as I have nerve issues with my hands, so the milliner's needles work for me for all of my hand work. But most quilters prefer the control that comes from using the shorter needles. With needles, the higher the number, the smaller the needle. So a size 12 needle is much smaller than a size 9 needle. Again, try a variety and keep extra needles in different sizes on hand.

As far as thread goes, select a variety of neutral-colored threads in several values. Dark gray, ivory, tan, black, and red will cover most of your piecing needs. You'll want to match the thread to the darker piece of fabric with which you're working. Also, use high-quality, all-cotton thread for your piecing. Threads in 50 or 60 weights are super thin and will disappear into your fabric as you stitch.

Using thread conditioner, such as Thread Heaven, results in for less tangling of your thread and smoother stitching. Conditioners are usually silicon-based and won't stain your fabrics.

Cut your thread up to 15 inches long. Anything longer and you'll wear out the thread from the friction caused by the sewing. It will also tangle less if you keep the length to 15 inches or less. If you have trouble threading the needle from one side, turn the needle over and try from the other side. Or use a needle threader if you find yourself frustrated. That's what they are made for, after all.

Question 108:
How do I piece by hand?

You can start your piecing by knotting your thread with a quilter's knot. Thread your needle and make one tail longer than the other. Hold your needle in your sewing hand parallel to the floor or table with the needle's point facing the opposite hand. Take the longer tail in your opposite hand and bring it to the needle, overlapping the thread onto the needle. It will look like one big loop. Hold the thread and the needle securely in your sewing hand and tightly wrap the thread over the needle four times with your opposite hand. With your sewing hand holding the loops in place, slowly pull the needle and thread through the loops until you reach the bottom of the longer tail. You should have a perfect knot sitting at the bottom of the thread. Trim the end ¼-inch below the knot and you're ready to go. This will take a little practice to perfect, but it's worth it.

You'll need to first determine the order of the piecing (many patterns will provide this information for you). Usually, blocks are first put together in units, and then the units are sewn into rows, and finally the rows are joined.

Pick up the first two pieces. Place the pieces right sides together. Your marked seam lines should clearly show. Place a pin at the start of the marked line through both pieces. (Check the other fabric to make sure the pin comes out in the correct spot.) Then, place another pin at the end of the marked line, checking once again on the other fabric. If the piece is big, feel free to add another pin or two to hold the pieces in place.

If you're right-handed, you'll work from right to left. If you're left-handed, you'll work from left to right. Starting at the appropriate pin, (left or right) remove it and replace it with your needle. Take one small stitch and gently pull the needle through the fabric on this first stitch until the knot stops your thread. Then, take several stitches onto your needle (this is called loading your needle) making your stitches small and checking the back of your unit to be sure you're following the marked seam line on both pieces. Gently pull the thread through the fabric until it stops, making sure to watch the thread's tension. If you pull too tightly on the thread, the fabric pieces will pucker. If it's too loose, the seam will not hold together. After you pull through the first set of stitches, place your needle into the start of the very last stitch you just made and then load your needle again. This creates a backstitch that will secure your thread.

Continue until you're at the end of the seam line, removing pins as you go along. If you're working with very small pieces, you may only need to load your needle once or twice.

When you reach the end of the marked seam line, leave your needle halfway out of the last stitch and wrap your thread around the needle twice. Pull the needle through the wrapped loops to create an end knot, and trim your thread. You've just finished your first piece.

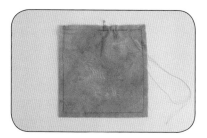

ABOVE Take one small stitch and gently pull the needle through the fabric on this first stitch until the knot stops your thread. Loading your needle, making your stitches small and check the back of your unit to be sure you're following the marked seam line on both pieces.

ABOVE Leave your needle halfway out of the last stitch and wrap your thread around the needle twice. Pull the needle through the wrapped loops to create an end knot, and trim your thread.

Question 109:
What is finger pressing?

Just like you won't be taking your sewing machine to work on your hand-piecing project on-the-go, you also won't have an iron with you. But

you can press pieced seams with your fingers and achieve enough flatness to continue your piecing. If you have fingernails, this is even easier to do.

After you've pieced your seam, fold the seam allowance to whichever side you want it to lay and flip your pieced unit rightside up. Take your finger or fingernail and gently crease the seam from the front several times. Remember that your body's temperature is 98 degrees (give or take a little), and this is enough heat to set your seams.

Question 110:
What about those odd angles, like Y-seams and curves?

I believe it's easier to tackle the unusual seams and angles with hand piecing than by machine. Because you need to really be able to get into the corners, you have greater maneuverability with a small hand needle than with a bulky sewing machine.

To succeed with the angles, start by making sure that your template is cut out as accurately as possible. Make sure you mark your lines as close to the template as possible and then sew along these lines accurately. As with all hand piecing, check the other piece of fabric often to ensure you are sewing along that piece's marked line. And only sew to the end of the marked line, not beyond it.

You might find pinning the straight angles difficult. Try working with smaller pins or don't use the pins and be very careful to check your stitching line against the marked line often.

For curves, pins will become your lifesaver. Use as many pins as needed to hold the pieces in place. In most traditional curved piecing, one piece of fabric will remain flat and the other may need to be clipped for successful piecing. The concave piece, which has an outside curve, will usually need a few clips to make it spread open. The clips are tiny snips from the fabric's outside edge to just before the marked/stitching line. Don't clip past the line! This will create a hole in the piece. How many clips you need depends on the size of the piece and if the curve is slight or extreme. Start with a couple and see if you can pin it well to the flat piece. If not, add a couple more clips. Then start piecing along the marked lines, removing pins as you work. When done, press your seam with your fingers and make sure there are no small puckers hiding in the seam.

12

APPLIQUÉ

Question 111:
What tools do I need for my appliqué project?

The answer here depends on what kind of appliqué technique you plan on using for your project. There are many different kinds of appliqué technique and several variations on those as well. As with everything else in quilting, find what works best for you, your skill level, and the project, and stick with it. Here is a sampling of the most popular techniques, which will get you through most projects, but I encourage you to explore other techniques in more detailed books on appliqué.

For all appliqué, you'll need:
• Small scissors
• Patterns
• Background blocks or fabric
• Fabrics for the appliqué pieces
• Pins for holding pieces in place

For needle-turn and reverse appliqué, add:
• An assortment of hand needles
• Thread: matched to the appliqué pieces' colors
• Marking pens/pencils
• Template plastic or freezer paper

For fusible appliqué, add:
• Fusible webbing
• Permanent extra-fine line marker
• Paper scissors
• Thread for top stitching
• Appliqué pressing sheet

For machine appliqué, add:
• Freezer paper
• Marking pens/pencils
• Appliqué glue
• Thread: matched to the appliqué pieces' colors

Question 112:
What is needle-turn hand appliqué?

Needle-turn is a fast way to achieve hand appliqué. In the method I use, take an appliqué pattern and trace it to the right side of a piece of fabric. You can make the tracing by using template plastic with the pattern drawn on it, cut out the shape and then trace it onto the fabric with a pencil or other washable marking pen. Or, trace the shape onto the dull side of freezer paper, cut out the piece exactly on the lines, then iron the freezer paper to the fabric's right side using a hot, dry iron.

With both methods, trim the appliqué piece leaving at least a ¼-inch seam allowance around the traced shape. You may need to trim this down more, but start with the ¼-inch.

If you have curves and inset points, clip them accordingly (see Questions 118 and 119). Match your appliqué thread as closely as possible to the dominant color of the appliqué piece. You'll want to use the thinnest and best quality thread available for sewing your appliqué down. Many quilters swear by silk thread, which is strong and practically invisible when sewn into the appliqué, but it can be hard to find. If you can find 50-weight cotton thread in a variety of colors, use that instead.

Your needle selection is similar to the needle choices for hand piecing. Refer back to the choices in Question 107.

Pin your appliqué piece to the background fabric, right-side up. Turn under your first edge. You'll be turning the fabric to its back-side just along the marked edge. You can

1   Draw the pattern onto template plastic, cut out and then trace it onto the fabric, right-side up, using a pencil or washable marking pen.

2   Pin your appliqué piece to the background fabric, right-side up.

3   Bring the knotted thread up from the back of the background fabric, catching a couple of threads.

use the needle's length and point to gently push the edge under and your finger to press or hold it in place as you work. Then, blind stitch the appliqué piece in place. With a blind stitch, the knotted length of thread comes up the back of the background fabric catching a thread or two along the folded edge of the appliqué piece. The thread then goes back down just into the background fabric along the piece's edge and comes up again about an 1/8-inch to the left of the previous stitch. As you work along the appliqué piece's edge, you'll turn the fabric under as you go, using your pointed tool to help where needed. With practice, needle-turn appliqué looks very nice and professional. You do not need to cut away the fabric behind the appliqué pieces, as some quilters do. It weakens the top and isn't necessary, even if you're hand quilting your top.

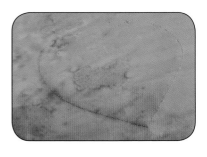

4 You do not need to cut away the fabric behind the appliqué pieces, as some quilters do. It weakens the top and isn't necessary, even if you're hand quilting your top.

5 The finished product.

Question 113:
What is fusible appliqué?

Fusible appliqué uses a fusible web that, when heated with the iron, melts and acts as a glue between two layers of fabric. I use Steam-a-Seam or Lite Steam-a-Seam for my appliqué work as it is lightweight and easy to work with, but there are many types of fusibles available to try.

Fusibles come in sheets and on the bolt and are protected by paper on one or both sides. The paper

1 Trace the shape onto one side of the paper.

should be transparent enough to allow you to trace the appliqué images on the paper. Remember that when you trace the pattern, you will be working in the reverse.

Trace the shape onto one side of the paper and roughly cut it out, leaving the tracing intact. Then, put the fusible side down on the appliqué fabric's wrong side and iron into place with the iron to the

2 Roughly cut it out, leaving the tracing intact.

4 Trim the piece along the traced lines of the paper and remove the paper.

3 Then, put the fusible side down on the appliqué fabric's wrong side and iron into place with the iron to the paper side.

5 Place the appliqué piece where indicated on the background fabric and iron in place, following the manufacturer's directions.

paper side. Trim the piece along the traced lines of the paper and remove the paper. The appliqué piece will now have the fusible on its wrong side. Place the appliqué piece where indicated on the background fabric and iron in place, following the manufacturer's directions. You now have a permanent bond between the two fabrics, but you still should do some sort of edge stitching to prevent the appliqué piece from unraveling over time.

There are several popular quilt designers who have made their whole career from fusible appliqué work. McKenna Ryan of Pine Needles and Letitia Hutchings of Mount Redoubt Designs are two designers whose quilt patterns are available almost everywhere.

Question 114:
What are some ways to handle raw edges?

Fusible appliqué creates raw edges along the appliqué piece's edge. There are several ways to finish the edges so the piece won't unravel with repeated use and washing.

The most common method of handling raw edges is to satin-stitch along every exposed edge. A satin stitch is a very tight zigzag stitch that can become its own design element. If you use the exact same color thread as the appliqué piece, the stitch's texture becomes the design element. If you use a contrasting thread, the color becomes the design element. When you're working the satin stitch around the appliqué pieces, you'll need to pivot around

curves and at corners. If you're working on satin-stitching points, thin out the satin stitch as you approach the point's end.

A satin stitch's width is determined by the size of the piece you're stitching in place. If you have a tiny piece, a wide satin stitch is going to overwhelm the appliqué. If you're working with too small a stitch, that will fade into the appliqué. Make sure the satin stitch's width is split in half between the appliqué piece and the background piece. You also might have to adjust your thread's tension to a slightly looser setting to avoid creating a tunnel from your stitching.

Another option for finishing your appliqué's edges is the blanket or buttonhole stitch, either by hand or machine. The machine version works just as well and it can be done much faster. Usually, a blanket stitch is made in contrasting thread (embroidery floss and pearl cotton are two good choices) so it stands out against the fabric.

To make the stitch by hand, bring the thread up along the appliqué edge, on the background side, from the back of the piece. Then, take your needle and run it perpendicular to the appliqué edge. Place the needle in about a ¼ inch away from the edge and bring it up at the edge, about a ¼ inch to the left of your starting point, before you bring the thread all the way out, loop the loose tail where your needle comes up along the appliqué edge. This secures your appliqué piece.

Your last choice for handling raw edges in fusible appliqué is to free-motion stitch a straight stitch just along the inside edge of the appliqué shape. This can be invisible by using invisible or matching threads, or you can use contrasting threads to show them off. This gives a raw look to the piece and can provide lots of texture if you have a lot of appliqué pieces to stitch.

ABOVE A satin stitch is a very tight zigzag stitch that can become its own design element.

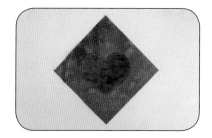

ABOVE Usually, a blanket stitch is made in contrasting thread (embroidery floss and pearl cotton are two good choices) so it stands out against the fabric.

ABOVE Your last choice for handling raw edges in fusible appliqué is to free motion stitch a straight stitch just along the inside edge of the appliqué shape.

Question 115:
What is machine appliqué?

In machine appliqué, you turn under the appliqué piece's edges before you stitch the piece down to the background. When you do your stitching, you're probably working with invisible thread and a tiny zigzag or blind hem stitch that becomes invisible in the work.

There are many ways to successfully turn under the edges of the pieces. I use freezer paper. Trace the appliqué image in reverse onto the freezer paper's dull size. Trim it along the traced line. With a hot, dry iron, iron the freezer paper, shiny-side down, onto the wrong side of your appliqué fabric. Cut out the appliqué shape leaving a ⅛-inch to ¼-inch seam allowance around the piece. Clip your curves as needed. With your iron and a stiletto or other thin, pointed tool, fold over the edges onto the back of the appliqué piece. Some quilters prefer using starch at this point to wet the edge and then iron it in place. Others use an appliqué glue to hold the turned-under edges in places. Others just rely upon the iron's heat to do the job.

Once the piece is prepared with its edges turned under, pin it to the background fabric and carefully edge stitch the piece to the background using a small zigzag stitch or blind hem stitch, which catches the turned-under appliqué piece's edge.

Question 116:
What is reverse appliqué?

In reverse appliqué, the background fabric is cut away and stitched under to reveal another fabric beneath it. Reverse appliqué works well with curves, offering another option for tackling those challenging swirls and circles.

Using your template pattern for the appliqué shape, trace the shape onto the right side of the background fabric using a pencil or washable marking pen. Slip the point of your small, sharp scissors into the center of the shape and cut the center out, leaving a ¼ inch or less from the marked edge. If you have curves, clip them just to the marked line. Pin the contrasting fabric under the background fabric to hold it in place. Working similarly to the needle-turn technique described in Question 112, turn under and blind stitch the edges of the marked shaped. When done, your new background fabric will be exposed and framed by the appliqué shape.

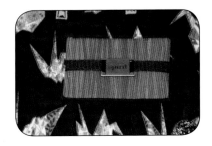

ABOVE In this example of reverse applique, the black fabric is cut away and stitched down to reveal the pink fabric underneath.

Question 117:
What is *broderie perse*?

Broderie perse (Persian embroidery) is the French term for a type of appliqué in which pre-printed images are cut from fabric and then sewn down onto another background fabric. Examples of *broderie perse* pop up in very old quilts of many different styles, such as antique Medallion quilts. Working with fusible appliqué and some type of edge finishing stitch is your best way to handle *broderie perse*.

　　Broderie perse is a fun project to do with kids. Have them make collage quilts by putting fusible webbing on the backs of novelty fabrics, cutting out different images, laying them on a background fabric, and ironing in place. You can quilt

the collage as you would any other quilt and your kids, or grandkids, can claim their own quilt to their credit.

BELOW The fish on this quilt were carefully cut from a single piece of printed fabric and then fused to this quilt's top, creating the *broderie perse* technique.

Question 118:
How do I handle curves?

Curves in appliqué do not need to cause stress. It's easy enough to learn to work with curves when you need to turn under the edges, either in needle-turn, reverse, or machine appliqué. There will be two kinds of curves you will face in your work: concave curves and convex curves. Concave curves are inward turning curves (think cave), convex curves bow outward.

For concave curves, a series of tiny clips/cuts into the fabric from the outside edge to just before the marked line will help the fabric fold over nicely. If you have a very sharp curve to work with, clips every ¼-inch or so should help. As you fold the clipped edge over, finger press it in place. You can also iron it flat on the wrong side of the appliqué piece. If you're using freezer paper, this is easier to do with the freezer paper's edge providing enough resistance to allow the folded edge to stop.

For convex curves that are not extreme, you should be able to trim the edge down to ⅛ inch and then turn it under as you work your blind stitches along the edges. If you have very tight convex curves, or you're working with circles, you might have

to resort to seam-allowance basting. Using your freezer paper pattern on the wrong side of the appliqué piece and with a ¼-inch seam allowance cut around the shape, take a series of tiny running stitches just along the outside of the freezer paper along the full length of the curve or circle. Don't go too far out into the seam allowance. Knot the end of the fabric and carefully draw the thread to close the seam allowance in and around the freezer paper pattern. Finger press the seam allowance in place and then iron down, making sure there are no tiny tucks or puckers along the edge. Remove the freezer paper. Then place the piece on your background fabric and machine or hand stitch into place.

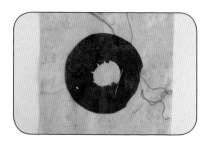

ABOVE For concave curves, a series of tiny clips/cuts into the fabric from the outside edge to just before the marked line will help the fabric fold over nicely.

Question 119:
How do I handle points?

You'll face inside points and outside points in your appliqué. Again, neither should cause you stress.

For inside points, you will need to clip straight into the point just short of the freezer paper pattern or marked line. This will allow you to turn under the edges without a problem.

Outside points are a little trickier. You'll turn under the point's right-side edge along the length of the line. At the point's tip, you'll see a bit of the turned-under edge sticking out. Stitch all the way to the fold's end and take an extra stitch at the end point for added stability. You can trim that bit sticking out a little (snip carefully so you're not cutting into your appliqué piece!), and then take your stiletto or finger and work the remaining bit under the appliqué piece and smooth in place. Finger press the seam firmly down and continue blind stitching.

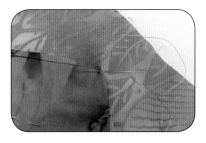

2   Stitch all the way to the fold's end and take an extra stitch at the end point for added stability.

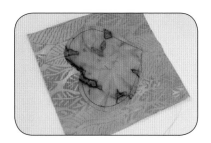

1   You'll turn under the point's right-side edge along the length of the line. At the point's tip, you'll see a bit of the turned-under edge sticking out.

3   Take your stiletto or finger and work the remaining bit under the appliqué piece and smooth in place.

13
ROWS AND BORDERS

Question 120:
What's the best way to mark rows?

I tend to do things unconventionally. That includes marking my quilt rows. When I'm finished with all of the blocks or pieces of my quilt and it's ready to be assembled, I arrange the whole thing on my carpeted floor. If you have a design wall, this probably works better, but I don't have a large enough design wall for my quilts, so the floor it is. If I'm working from a pattern, the block or quilt arrangement is probably already known and I just spread it out as needed. If I'm working on my own design, or need to tweak the pattern, I arrange and rearrange the pieces until I'm happy. This might mean that I leave it overnight and check it in the morning. As with writing, quilting can benefit from a well-rested brain.

Once I know how my quilt is to be arranged, I work from the top left corner of the quilt and use note paper and pins to mark my rows. The top row is 1 and the left side is where I start. I pin the Post-It marked "1" to the first block and then pick up the rest of the blocks in the row, in order, placing each new block under "1." I make sure not to turn or twist the blocks, even slightly, as I need to sew them in order. This stack becomes Row 1.

I continue this process to the bottom of the quilt making sure the stacking is completely consistent. If I think I may have trouble with the directions of the blocks, I will also add a north/up pointing arrow to the note paper to show the direction in which the blocks are to be held and assembled. I leave the note paper in place until the entire top is sewn together, just in case I need the reference for something else.

Question 121:
How do I sew rows together?

You really need to use your pins at this point, even if you don't like them. As each row is completed, lay them on the floor or design wall right-side up, in order, from quilt top to bottom. Assuming you have a traditional quilt made with blocks that will be set together, you'll need to iron your seams for Row 1 all in one direction, then iron the seams for Row 2 in the opposite direction. Continue alternating the seams' directions to the last row. Replace each row after you iron the seams.

With the rows pressed and facing you in the correct order, take Row 1 and flip it over, wrongside up, onto Row 2. You won't have to move Row 2 at all. Both rows are now right sides facing together. It's time to start pinning. If you've ironed the seams correctly, Row 1's seams should be nicely nestled with Row 2's seams (see Question 93.) You need to pin at each intersection of these nestled seams, as well as at the start and end of the rows.

Most blocks will be big enough to warrant another pin or two between the seams' intersections. You'll be pinning so that Row 1 is facing up.

After you've pinned your rows, bring the rows to your machine and with Row 1 facing up, backstitch the end for about an inch and then stitch forward, removing the pins as you stitch along and being careful not to stitch over the pins. Go slowly and make sure you're following the ¼-inch seam allowance guides. When you reach the end of the row, backstitch again and remove the joined rows.

Bring the rows to the ironing board and iron the seam you've just sewn, in one direction. It won't matter which direction, but be consistent in the direction as you add rows to the quilt's top.

Continue to add rows, one at a time, to the bottom of the sewn rows. You should always pin the new row to the existing set of rows, and you'll be sewing from this direction as well. So Row 3 will be pinned and sewn to Row 2, Row 4 to Row 3, and so on until you're finished with your rows.

Question 122:
What is sashing?

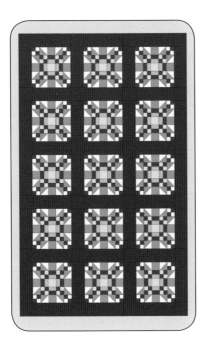

Sashing is the strips of fabric, sometimes pieced together, that separate and/or frame the blocks. Not all quilts have sashing, but sashing is a very useful design element for airing out the blocks and adding more length or width to a quilt.

When sashing is pieced, you can create a secondary design in the quilt's top. There is no set size for sashing, but you want it to enhance the overall effect of the quilt's design. If sashing is too wide, it can take away from the blocks' impact.

LEFT Sashing is used to separate the blocks in a quilt's design.

Question 123:
How do I set blocks on-point?

Setting your blocks on-point means the block is turned on the diagonal, at a 45-degree angle. For many blocks, just doing this quarter turn makes the design completely different.

Because you're removing the straight-line ease from the design, you'll need to fill in the sides with triangles, if you're going to turn your on-point into a straight-edged quilt. You'll have two kinds of triangles to deal with: the corner triangles and the side triangles.

There are fancy formulas for determining the size of the triangles, and frankly the fractions become minute and unwieldy, so a chart is simpler. You'll be cutting the squares and then either making one or two cuts diagonally to make two or four triangles, respectively. These square sizes are rounded to the nearest $1/2$ inch and you will need to trim the side triangles within a $1/4$ inch of the edges of the on-point blocks. Do this after you've pieced all of the blocks with the side triangles by lining up your rotary ruler to the block's points and trimming the triangles' excess to the points. For the corner triangles, use a corner rotary ruler to square up the corners to the on-point blocks and trim. Then you can add borders as desired.

Finished Block	Square for corner triangles (one cut)	Square for side triangles (two cuts)
4"	4"	7 $1/2$"
5"	5"	8 $1/2$"
6"	5 $1/2$"	10 $1/2$"
7"	6"	11 $1/2$"
8"	7"	13"
9"	7 $1/2$"	14 $1/2$"
10"	8 $1/2$"	16"
11"	9"	17"
12"	10"	18 $1/2$"
13"	10 $1/2$"	20"
14"	11"	21 $1/2$"
15"	12"	23"

Question 124:
What are borders?

Borders are fabric strips that frame the assembled quilt blocks or top. They can be simple or decorative. Most are straight, but some are curved or scalloped. A border can be a series of different fabrics framing the quilt. A border can also be made up of pieced or appliquéd sections that surround the center.

There are some quilts that are made much better by the border, whether from the design or the quilting within the border. Don't discount the quilt's border when you're working on your design. It's as important a part of the overall quilt as the blocks.

BELOW Borders frame a quilt's design.

Question 125:
How do I make a straight-cut border?

The inclination for joining borders to a quilt top is usually to cut lengths of border strip at the width you desire, sew the lengths to the border until it extends beyond the edge of the quilt top, and then trim the corners to meet the edges.

This sometimes results in a wavy border because your quilt's measurements are slightly off throughout the top. Instead, measure the quilt top through the middle, length, and width.

If possible, cut the border strips from the fabric length, parallel to the selvage. That way you can avoid piecing border strips. If you need to cut from the fabric's width and piece the border strips to accommodate the quilt's length, use a ¼-inch seam and make sure your pieces are cut very straight.

Start with the measurement for the quilt's length and cut two strips of border fabric at that length by the width of the border plus the seam allowance. Pin the borders to the top. This is important as you might need to ease in the borders to the quilt. Easing is a dressmaker's technique where a slightly shorter fabric is pinned to a slightly longer piece of fabric, then gently stretched while sewn to ease it into the longer piece. Sew the borders to the quilt's lengths. Iron the seams to the border.

For the quilt's width, take the width measurement and add in the size of the border's widths and subtract 1 inch (for the seam allowances). Pin the borders in place and sew, easing where needed. Iron the seams to the border and your top is ready for sandwiching and quilting. You can add as many borders as you'd like, one at a time, using this method. Many quilts feature double borders of differing sizes as a design element.

BELOW A straight-cut border is the simplest to achieve. Strips are sewn to two parallel sides, and then the second set of strips are sewn to the opposite parallel sides.

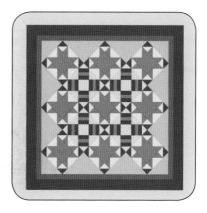

Question 126:
How do I make a border with corner squares?

ABOVE Corner squares offer a design alternative to the simple squared-off border arrangement. Using a contrasting fabric, or even a small quilt block in the sqaure, helps jazz up the overall design. The secret bonus is it's an easy way to add a border, far simpler than working with mitered corners! But don't tell anyone.

Corner squares are a nice way to add additional interest to a border, and if you happen to have four leftover blocks from your project, you can use those to good effect.

Measure your quilt's center lengthwise and widthwise. Cut (and piece if needed) border strips for the length and width. Cut four corner squares using the width measurement of the borders. If your border is 6 $\frac{1}{2}$ inches by 40 inches, your corner square will be 6 $\frac{1}{2}$-inches square. Sew the first two border strips to the quilt, left and right side. Then, to the border top, sew a corner square to each end of the border strip. Repeat for the bottom border strip. Pin the top and bottom borders in place making sure the intersections line up and sew in place.

Question 127:
How do I make a mitered border?

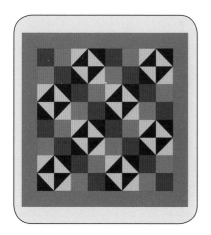

ABOVE Once you master a mitered border (and it won't take long), you will look like an expert quilter without even breaking a sweat. Mitered borders are also fun to make, using several different border rows, giving a striped effect to the border design.

Mitered borders add a wonderful touch to a quilt's edges, especially when you're working with a fabric that has a directional or large print you want to emphasize. They take a little practice to get right, but they're worth the time.

Decide on the width of your border. Then calculate the length of your border strips by measuring through the middle of the quilt, top to bottom and side to side. Add to those numbers (for top/bottom and sides) the border's width times two, and cut (and possibly piece) the border strips to those lengths. Then, add 4 inches to that number and cut/piece your border strips. If you want a 6-inch border and your lengthwise measurement is 50 inches, you'll cut or piece a 6-inch by 66-inch border.

Find the center of your borders and the centers of each side of your quilt top. Pin the top/bottom borders to the quilt top, matching the centers, right sides together. Sew from end to end, stopping a ¼-inch short of each end. Iron the seams out to the borders. Add the side borders in the same way.

Bring your quilt to the ironing board. At one corner, extend the border out and press. For the overlapping border, fold the end under at a 45-degree angle on top of the extended border and pin in place. (Use a square ruler to make sure the corner is squared.) Use a blind stitch to tack the angled border down to the extended border. Then trim the seam allowance and press the seam open.

14

PREPARING YOUR TOP
FOR QUILTING

Question 128:
How do I calculate the backing yardage?

Backing is the third layer for your quilt sandwich. You can be fancy with the backing and splurge on matching fabric. You can buy extra-wide backing fabric so no piecing will be involved. You can also use large scraps leftover from your project and piece a backing together. What is important is that you have a backing of some kind for your quilt.

- Make sure you calculate your measurements with an extra 2 inches around the quilt top to allow for any take-up in the quilting.
- If your quilt is 40 inches or fewer along two sides, you'll only need one length of backing fabric to cover the other measurement.
- If your quilt is larger, measure the entire quilt. Regardless of your quilt's orientation, take the smaller measurement and work from that.

If the measurement is between 41 inches and 80 inches, you'll need two lengths of fabric to cover the back. If your measurement of the narrower side is between 80 inches and 120 inches, you'll need three lengths. Almost all quilts will fall into these ranges.

- To determine the yardage needed, take the longer side and divide by 36. Whatever the number is, round to the nearest 1/2 yard. Multiply that number by how many lengths you need and that is your yardage.

Here's the math for a quilt that is 72 inches wide by 96 inches long: 72 inches wide needs two lengths of fabric. 96 divided by 36 is 2.66. Rounded to the nearest 1/2 yard totals three yards. Double that for the lengths needed and it will take six yards to cover the quilt's back.

Question 129:
How do I piece my backing?

While there is no set method to piece backing, you probably want to maximize the fabric you have. Let's assume you have all the fabric you need. The easiest thing to do until you're comfortable with the math involved is to sketch out a piecing plan for the back.

Draw the outline of the quilt's dimensions on paper and label the inch count of each side. Figure your backing fabric at 40 inches wide, take the narrowest sides and divide that by 40. This is how many lengths of fabric you'll need for the backing. If your back is 70 inches wide, you'll need two lengths of the backing fabric. You'll sew one seam down the middle of two pieces of the backing fabric and trim the sides down later.

You can work from the long side as well. If your quilt is 100 inches wide along that side, you'll need three lengths of fabric to cover the back. It doesn't matter which way you work, as long as there is enough fabric to do the job.

Some quilters, in the interest of saving material and using up what they have, will piece large pieces of fabric together to use up big scraps. Again, this is a numbers game and you'll need to calculate what to sew and what you need, and this is most easily accomplished using a sketch with your measurements.

If you're looking for an alternative to piecing backings, especially for large quilts, there are many choices on the quilt market for extra-wide cotton backings made for quilts. At about 109 inches, these fabrics will cover almost every quilt you will make, in one piece. Remember to make sure you have at least 2 inches extra all around when you trim your backing. When asking or searching for these fabrics, ask for "extra-wide quilt backing" and you should be able to find many to choose from.

BELOW Illustration to show backing piecing options.

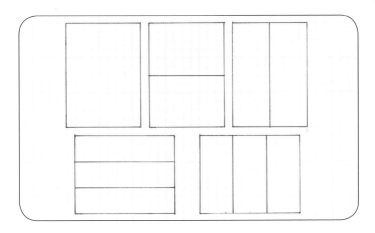

Question 130:
What kind of batting should I use?

Like prewashing and hand needles, the type of batting used is a personal decision, based on the project's needs and the quilter's preferences.

Battings are made from an assortment of materials, including cotton, polyester, wool, silk, bamboo, and, most recently, recycled soda bottles. (I kid you not!) Some wool and cotton battings require prewashing, but there are plenty of brands available that don't if you prefer to skip this step.

You must first decide how you will quilt your quilt. Different techniques have different batting requirements. The techniques include hand quilting, machine quilting, and tying the quilt. A batting that works great for hand quilting may not be the best choice for machine quilting.

Also, you need to know your preference and the quilt's final use. If the quilt will be hung, you probably don't want a very fluffy batting. If your quilt will be snuggled under, a fluffier batting makes more sense. Wool battings add actual warmth to the quilt's effect. Polyester batting can also be warm to lie under. All-cotton battings tend to be breathable and might be a good warm-weather batting.

You also will want to consider how dense your quilting will be. Some battings recommend quilting every 2 inches; others can have the quilting spaced out up to 10 inches. This makes a big difference to the overall quilting plan you might have in mind. Most battings will have the recommended quilt spreads printed on the wrapper.

If, as a beginner, you're looking for a good all-around batting to get you started in what is a marketplace rich with options, turn to all-cotton, needle-punched battings, especially the kinds that don't require pre-washing. Cotton battings look flatter and more traditional than other choices.

For whatever batting you try, make a test sandwich where you've quilted the batting in the technique you prefer. Make sure to write on the test sandwich what the batting was. This personal reference library of batting will help you as you progress with your quilting skills. You can refer back to them as you narrow your batting needs.

Question 131:
How do I make a quilt sandwich?

A traditional quilt sandwich is composed of the quilt top, batting, and backing layers. Most quilters cut the batting and backing 2 inches beyond the edges of the top. This provides enough extra room to accommodate any constriction during the quilting. If your top measures 50 inches by 70 inches, your batting/backing layers need to be at least 54 inches by 74 inches. You'll trim the excess when you're done with the quilting.

Follow the guidelines for determining the backing yardage and piecing in Questions 128 and 129. Make sure that the backing and top are ironed as smoothly as possible. You don't want any puckers or crinkles.

Make the sandwich by laying the backing right-side down on a large enough surface. For smaller quilts, this is simple to do on a dining table. Larger quilts take more room. Some quilters use folding tables, others, like me, use their floors. Many local quilt shops will allow quilters to use their classroom space to sandwich quilts. They may not allow the use of spray baste, though.

Once the backing layer is spread out completely on a surface, wrong-side up, lay the batting on top of it. Most batting will come large enough to cover the backing. The exception could be a king-sized quilt where you might need to stitch together pieces of batting to accommodate the width. This is usually done by hand with a simple X stitch on the overlap, which is then trimmed down as closely as possible to the stitching to avoid creating too much bulk where the backing is joined. Spread the batting from the center outward on the backing. It's important that the batting is as smooth as possible.

The quilt top comes next. If your top is big, you may need an extra set of hands to help you open up the quilt top and lay it correctly on top of the batting. Again, make sure it's well-pressed, that the seams are all flat and in the correct direction. If your seams are poorly pressed, it will create added bulk.

Spread out the top on the batting, smoothing out from the center to the edges, and you're ready to baste in a traditional manner (thread or pins as follows). If you're spray-basting, you'll handle this order a little differently.

Question 132:
How do I thread-baste a quilt?

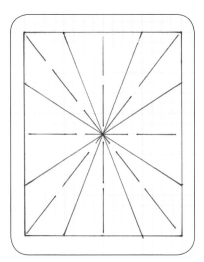

LEFT This illustration is showing thread basting.

Once the sandwich is complete, you're ready to baste your quilt. The oldest, most traditional way to baste the quilt is with needle and thread. Thread-basting is best for projects that will be hand quilted.

Place the quilt sandwich, top-side up, on a firm surface. Use the longest needle you have and any thread (since it won't be staying in your quilt), start from one corner and stitch long stitches (at least 12 inches apart) diagonally until you reach the opposite corner. The firm surface will offer leverage for your needle. Repeat on the other corners. Then stitch a cross through the quilt's north-south and east-west sections. If your quilt is really big, you'll probably need to do more west. The goal is to bisect the quilt until there are very few areas that are not secured with thread.

After you've quilted your quilt, you should be able to pull the long basting threads out of the quilt.

Question 133:
How do I pin-baste a quilt?

Place the sandwich on a firm surface. You'll also need enough large, rust-proof safety pins to place a pin about every 2 to 3 inches around the quilt.

Pinning can be very hard on your fingers. But, as with most quilting dilemmas, there are tools on the market to help you close the pins.

After your quilt is pin-basted, you can quilt as desired, but you must remove the pins before you stitch over them. This takes more time away from your quilting, but it's a solid alternative to the thread-basting technique.

Question 134:
How do I spray-baste a quilt?

Spray baste is a temporary adhesive designed to work with fabric. It sprays from a can and can be washed out. I use 505 Spray and Fix religiously. It's acid-free and won't gum up your sewing machine needle. There are other brands on the market, but I'm loyal to 505. I've never had a problem with it and the smell of some of the other sprays is too harsh for me.

The reasons I prefer spray baste are: It takes minutes to baste even a king-size quilt; the adhesive lasts forever—you only need to reactivate it with a steam iron; it's repositionable, so if your sandwich has a pucker in it, you can lift and re-smooth the sandwich; you can let your quilt sit for years without worrying about the spray basting wearing off (yes, I've tested this); and, it provides the best possible surface for machine quilting because every part of the sandwich has evenly adhered to itself.

Basting with spray baste works a little differently, and the instructions provided here differ from what the manufacturer recommends. But it's worked for me for years and I stick with it.

You'll need a well-ventilated room or area to work in. I use the floor of my sewing studio. The carpet is commercial grade and trashed—I don't care about it too much anymore. I have another friend who sets up folding banquet tables in her garage and leaves the garage door open. Just makes sure that well-ventilated doesn't mean wind- or fan-driven air. You don't want to blow the spray chemicals into your face! If you're sensitive to the spray baste's smell, use a face mask.

Start by laying your backing fabric, wrong-side up, on your firm surface. Make sure the backing is smooth. Then, lay your batting on top of the backing. When they are both smoothed out, peel the batting halfway back onto itself. This exposes half of the backing's wrong side and half of the batting's right side. Hold the spray baste can about 12 inches above the fabric and with a light touch, spray the entire exposed surfaces of both the backing and the batting. Do this quickly and evenly, making sure there is an extra moment of spray for the corners of the quilt sandwich. Then, carefully and slowly, smooth the batting onto the wrong side of the backing. Work with your hand flat, smoothing from the center to the edges. When done, repeat with the other half of the backing.

Once the backing and batting are bonded, carefully lay the top, wrong-side down, onto the batting. Again, make sure you have the seams all well-ironed in place. If you need an extra pair of hands, enlist help. The batting/backing combo still needs to be at least an extra 2 inches larger all around than the top. Once the top is in place, fold the top back onto itself halfway. Spray evenly and quickly, covering the exposed batting and the top's

wrong side. Then, same as with the batting/backing section, smooth the top back onto the batting, from the center out to the edges. Repeat with the other half of the top.

When you're done with the sandwich, take it to the ironing board and iron the entire sandwich, from the center outward, with a hot steam iron. This "sets" the fabric in place and makes the adhesive adhere well. From this point forward you can take as much or as little time as you want to quilt your project. If the sandwich seems to split apart at some point in the future, just take it back to your steam iron and reactive the adhesive.

Some quilters swear that spray baste gums up their sewing machine needles. I've noticed that yes, there's a little gumming with the needles, but it happens around the same time I'd be changing the needle anyway. The time- and labor-saving benefits far outweigh tossing the needles for me.

Question 135:
How do I keep my quilt flat?

If ever there was one factor in a quilt that separates the amateur from the pro, it's how the quilt hangs when it's displayed.

A quilt that has wavy edges looks unprofessional. But, I admit

that it's hard to achieve a quilt that's completely flat. A flat quilt comes from a combination of accurate piecing, even and balanced quilting, smooth sandwiching, good trimming, and perfect binding. When you've achieved all of this, and add a sleeve that's put on correctly, your quilt should hang straight and proud. If you're slightly wavy at the end of your work, you can try to iron your quilt well with a hot steam iron.

This acts as a blocking method of sorts and can amend some of the issues. If you're not handling an art quilt that should never meet water, wash it first as well and then iron.

Question 136:
What other fabrics can I use for a quilt backing?

Flannel makes a wonderful backing for quilts, especially baby quilts and lap quilts. You must purchase extra yardage and prewash flannel, sometimes twice, because there is a very high shrinkage factor.

One of the nice things about using cotton flannel with a cotton, needle-punched batting is that over time and with much washing, the flannel and the batting almost seem to bond together, creating a very thick, dense and yet soft, backing for the quilt.

Microfleece is also wonderful to use on the backs of your quilts, but it's more difficult to work with.

Question 137:
How do I work with microfleece?

I love using microfleece as backings for quilts, especially children's quilts. But, to be honest, it's a pain to quilt. That's because the nature of microfleece makes it very squishy, for want of a better word. It moves and slides like a downhill skier! To combat this factor, spray-baste your microfleece to your batting or top.

(Some fleeces are so thick, you can opt not to use batting.) You'll need to smooth the layers out carefully. Then, once your sandwich is done, iron it well from the top only (so you don't ruin the fleece's nap) to smooth out any hidden puckers. You're ready to quilt as desired at this point.

HAND QUILTING

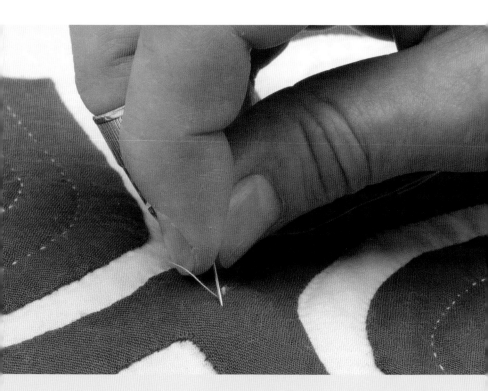

Question 138:
What do I need to know before starting to hand quilt?

Hand quilting, when done correctly, adds a beautiful soft texture to any quilt. It takes times to complete a hand quilt, but if you have the patience and enjoy handwork, hand quilting could be your preferred mode of quilting.

Every beginning quilter should try hand quilting at least one project. Quilting's roots come from hand work and, even if you decide it's not for you, the connection you make with traditional quilting will only enhance your understanding of the art and your connection with its history.

The tools for hand quilting mimic the tools used for hand piecing (see Question 105). You'll also need supplies for marking your quilt top.

Question 139:
How do I mark a quilt?

There are many different marking tools in the quilt world today; you only have to find what works for you.

Marking pens and pencils are the most popular. Many of these are erasable or washable. It's very important that you read and follow the directions for these tools. The ink of some pens disappears from the heat of the iron. The ink from others sets in the fabric by the heat of the iron. You don't want to spend all that time working on your project only to find the marks won't come out of the top.

If you're working with stencils, you can mark the stencil's lines in the quilt with marking pens and pencils, or with chalk bags. These bags tap powdered chalk onto the quilt's top through the stencil's open lines. You can also trace the stencil's lines with a chalk pencil. Again, this is a case of finding what works best for you.

Question 140:
How do I use quilting stencils?

It's said that the quilting makes the quilt. If that is true, a quilt stencil becomes a very important part of the quilting design. A stencil is usually a sheet of thin but sturdy plastic that has a design cut out of it. A quilting stencil can be simple or intricate but they always require some kind of marking to transfer the design to the quilt's top. There are literally hundreds, if not thousands, of stencils on the market. You'll need to pick stencils that enhance the look and feel of the quilt, and that are the appropriate size.

You'll find border designs, corner designs, medallion designs, and all-over designs. Make sure the design fits the area for which it is intended. If you have a 3-inch border, a 5-inch stencil pattern won't work.

BELOW Quilting stencils provide an easy and accurate way to mark designs on your quilt's top for guidance. They can also be made with blank stencil or template plastic and a craft knife.

Question 141:
What kind of needle do I need?

Most quilters use a between or sharps needle for quilting. In general, the smaller the needle, the finer the stitches. A size 10 or 12 needle is small enough to work your quilt stitching.

Just like with hand piecing (see Question 107), the kind of needle you prefer becomes a personal choice. Carry several different needles on you and try them all out at some point.

Question 142:
What sort of thread should I use?

All cotton-thread is the preferred thread for most hand quilting projects. You can use a high-quality thread and beeswax or thread conditioner, or you can buy pre-waxed quilting thread (Gutterman and JP Coats are two brands that come to mind) for your hand quilting. Silk and metallic threads may also be used successfully. Perle cotton is used in Sashiko quilting (Question 11).

Question 143:
How do I use a hoop or lap frame?

Quilting hoops look like oversized embroidery hoops. Lap frames are usually square. Both help to support the fabric as you perform your quilting stitch. Smaller than a floor frame, a hoop or lap frame can sit on your lap as you do your quilting.

When you use your quilting hoop or frame, your fabric is not taut and completely stretched out in the hoop. Instead, it's slightly loose, which allows ease of movement for the needle as it works through the fabric.

RIGHT To help prevent puckers and folds in your quilt while quilting, consider using a quilt frame or hoop to support your quilt sandwich.

Question 144:
Do I really need a frame or hoop for quilting?

It is possible to hand quilt without a hoop or frame. Using a thin batting and holding your quilt in your lap, you can "feed" the quilt onto your needle, several stitches at a time.

With time, you can achieve small stitches, but devoted hand quilters swear by the support gained from a hoop or frame.

Question 145:
How do I make a rocking stitch?

1   Start with your needle pointed straight down into the quilt sandwich's top. Your other hand should be underneath the sandwich.

2   Angle your needle and push into the sandwich while using your thumb to help "bump" the fabric where the stitch passes through. Push the needle slightly through the top.

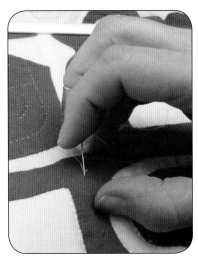

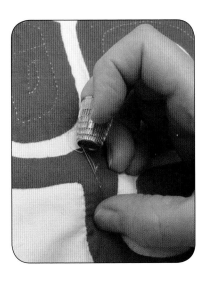

3   Again, put your needle into the top, straight down and then angle it up through the fabric with your thumb helping again. Push the needle slightly through the top.

4   Your quilt stitches will "gather" on the needle. This is called loading the needle. When several stitches are on the needle, pull it through and start again.

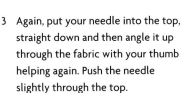

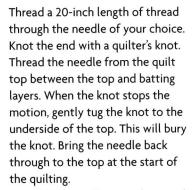

Thread a 20-inch length of thread through the needle of your choice. Knot the end with a quilter's knot. Thread the needle from the quilt top between the top and batting layers. When the knot stops the motion, gently tug the knot to the underside of the top. This will bury the knot. Bring the needle back through to the top at the start of the quilting.

Hold the needle point down and straight into the sandwich. Your less-dominant hand should be under the quilt and hoop on the quilt's backing. To make the rocking stitch, move your dominant hand at an angle so the needle goes into the quilt angled. At the same time, use your thumb from the same hand to push the fabric down in front of the needle, creating a bump in the quilt. Angle the needle so it is parallel to the quilt top and push through the bump. As soon as the needle appears in the bump, stop pushing and start a new stitch. Try to load the needle with about four stitches at a time to start. Pull the thread all the way through the quilt. Start again.

Question 146:
How small should the stitches be?

It's more important that your stitches be even in length than tiny. A beginning hand quilter should strive for consistency before any other factor is important. As you develop your hand quilting skills, you'll be able to make smaller stitches.

A master hand quilter consistently achieves between ten and fourteen stitches to the inch. If you're working at six to eight stitches per inch consistently, you're fine for now and your skills will increase with practice.

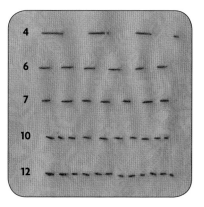

RIGHT It's more important to have consistent stitches than tiny stitches. The numbers here are the stitches per inch, and quilters use these numbers to determine the quality of the quilt stitch. The smaller the stitch, the "better" the stitch.

Question 147:
Do I really need a thimble?

Some quilters survive without the protection of a thimble on their fingers but with practice and the correct thimble, it's much easier to control the needle and the stitch when you wear one.

Thimbles are designed to have some "give" point on what would be your finger's pad. Traditional thimbles have dotted indentations on the pad, similar to how a golf ball's surface looks. These indentations give greater needle control to the stitcher.

Other thimbles made with soft materials such as rubber or leather help grip the needle to provide the control.

Thimbles come in all sorts of materials and sizes. Even if you have long fingernails, there's a thimble out there that you can use.

RIGHT Thimbles need to be snug, so have different sizes on hand for changing temperatures.

Question 148:
Are there alternatives to hand or machine quilting?

Yes, there are alternative ways to secure the three layers of your quilt sandwich together besides quilting,

BELOW Flowing from Dusk to Dawn. The river is "quilted" with pearl beads.

but most of the time, the quilting serves the quilt best.

You can tie a quilt with yarn, thread, buttons, or ribbons. You'll need to space the ties at close intervals to ensure the quilt stays

together during washing.

You can also embellish a quilt with beads or trinkets as another way to secure the layers.

For very small pieces/wall quilts, you can probably not quilt it at all and get away with it. But remember, the quilting adds dimension and texture to the quilt's surface.

Question 149:
I bought an unfinished antique quilt top. Should I finish it?

I checked with a certified quilt appraiser on this question. I have two unfinished antique quilts my great-great aunts left to me. One of them even has the needle with the thread still sticking in the top. I've never removed it, but have considered finishing the top. I was told that unless there is some strong, definitive value in the quilt maker's work, finishing the quilt will not affect it adversely.

Along those lines, I've seen many tops at quilt shows that are available for sale. I've known a few quilters who have adopted these tops and turned them into a finished quilt, either by traditional handquilting methods or by machine quilting. I think it's better for the quilt's integrity to be preserved by finishing it than by allowing it to sit unused for the rest of its existence.

It's become popular in recent years for enterprising crafters to use old, thread-bare quilts for other projects: clothing, pillows, stuffed animals, and other creative fabrications. I would not advise doing this unless you're absolutely sure the quilt's provenance (its maker and history) is unknown and that the quilt is in such poor condition that it would not survive whole otherwise.

But if you are sure you're not going to be haunted by the ghost of the quilt's maker for cutting it up, there are some wonderful projects you can use in old quilt pieces. Think about handbags, vests, and framed art made from old quilts.

MACHINE QUILTING

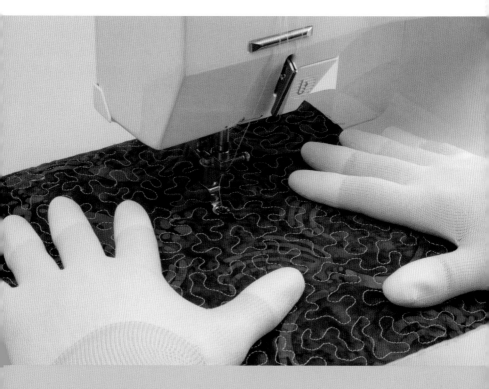

Question 150:
Why would I machine quilt my project?

Before the late 1980s, a quilt that was machine quilted would have shocked the sensibilities of quilt aficionados everywhere. Then, in 1989, art quilter Caryl Bryer Fallert entered her machine-quilted masterpiece, *Corona #2: Solar Eclipse*, into the American Quilter's Society show, won the $10,000 Best of Show award, and quilting never laughed at machine work again. Caryl's beautiful quilt ushered in a new era for modern quilters and machine quilting gloves were donned from that point forward.

Machine quilting has many advantages over hand quilting. The first is speed. You can finish a quilt in a fraction of the time it takes to work by hand. You also have more flexibility with thread effects. Metallic threads and variegated threads show up better in machine work. A quilt can be densely quilted when you use a machine, which is an effect that some quilters want in their work.

Machine quilting is fun! It takes practice and you need to know your tools, but once you learn how to control the quilt and your machine, you will enjoy the rhythmic motion of moving your quilt.

On the downside, machine quilting has some limitations. First, you need a sewing machine, and one that likes free-motion quilting. This doesn't mean you have to buy a new machine, but at times, your existing machine might well need some additional supplies or bobbin adjustments to accomplish your free-motion work.

Because you need a machine, machine quilting is not portable. Lastly, if you're working with free-motion machine quilting (see Question 151), be prepared to practice; the learning curve can be frustrating.

BELOW Corona #2: Solar Eclipse by Caryl Bryer Fallert, 1989.

Question 151:
What is free-motion machine quilting?

When you're working on straight lines for your machine quilting, you're probably using a walking foot and your feed dogs are up, or engaged. You're forced to direct the quilt in one direction under the needle and your quilting will be very orderly and simple. There is absolutely nothing wrong with this approach to your quilts and you'll be able to make beautiful quilts with just a straight stitch.

But, most modern sewing machines are capable of handling free-motion machine quilting. In free-motion work, your feed dogs are down (retracted) or covered so they don't move the fabric under the needle. Also, you're working with a darning foot or free-motion foot, which doesn't sit on top of the quilt while you sew. Instead, it moves up and down lightly on the

BELOW As your skills with free-motion quilting improve, the amount of fun and creativity you will experience will grow. Free-motion quilting feels like you're drawing with the sewing machine's needle.

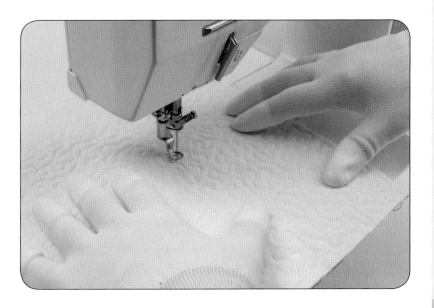

quilt's surface as you stitch. All of this enables you to freely move the quilt sandwich in any direction under the needle while the machine stitches. It's like drawing or doodling with your thread and it's a lot of fun to do. Master machine quilters can achieve all kinds of thread effects with their free-motion work. You can work with marked quilt patterns or you can wing it and just draw with your thread.

Question 152:
How do I prepare my quilt for machine quilting?

The basting information provided in Questions 132 to 134 applies for machine and hand quilting. I prefer to spray-baste my quilt for machine quilting because I don't worry that squishing my quilt to work it around the sewing machine bed will move the sandwich layers, and there are no pins to remove.

Question 153:
What materials do I need for machine quilting?

Besides the quilt sandwich, you will need several new machine needles of the appropriate size and type (see Question 157); thread for your quilt's top and bobbin; marking tools if you're working with stencils or more formal quilting effects; quilter's gloves or traction paddles for moving the quilt under the needle; a darning or free-motion foot for your free-motion work; a walking or even-feed foot for straight quilting; a single needle plate for your machine, if it's available; a machine extension table if your machine doesn't sit flush with your sewing table; extra bobbins; and extra lighting.

Some of these items are optional or may already be supplied with your sewing machine. But if you really enjoy machine quilting, having these tools and supplies will make the task much more fun.

Question 154:
What is a practice sandwich?

A practice sandwich (a prepared top, batting, and bottom layer; see Question 131) helps to do two things. First, it lets you test different combinations of thread, needles, and tension to determine what works best. As you stitch and evaluate your work, you'll be able to write on your sandwich what the tension setting and needle were that you used. That way you'll have a record of the settings that you can refer back to the next time you start quilting.

The other reason to have a practice sandwich is that most quilters benefit from a warm-up session before they start their free-motion machine quilting. This will loosen up your muscles and help smooth out your stitches.

You can even have two sandwiches, one for recording the stitches and one for warm-up.

Question 155:
What about the top thread?

These days you can pretty much use whatever top thread you like for your machine quilting, as long as you know with which needle and tension it works best.

The exception would be very thick or heavy threads that are specifically marked for "bobbin work." These threads provide a special effect from their thickness and they are only used in the bobbin.

Your best bet when starting to machine quilt is to use a high-quality cotton thread. For beginners, use a thread that will blend into the quilt. When you get better, you'll probably want to showcase your quilting more and then you can use contrasting thread colors. Look for 40- to 60-weight long-staple cotton threads. You'll want to buy at least two spools for a bed-sized quilt, just in case you run out of the thread. Variegated threads offer a slight dimension to the quilting and are fun to use. Their color changes can be subtle or dramatic, but they always offer a little something more to your quilt top.

If you have a lot of colors in your quilt, try a thread color that blends into all of them, probably in a medium tone.

Question 156:
What about the bobbin thread?

The best threads I've used for bobbins when I'm machine quilting are Bottom Line threads by machine quilter extraordinaire Libby Lehman (made by Superior Threads), and Aurifil's line of 60-weight cotton threads.

Bottom Line is a 60-weight long-staple polyester thread that runs through the bobbin like a hot knife through butter. Because it's a synthetic, the lint is much less. And best of all, because the thread is so thin, you can wind more onto a bobbin, which means fewer bobbin changes. Aurifil is similar to Bottom Line with performance, but it's cotton. Choose a bobbin thread color that blends into the quilt's backing. You don't need to show off the back of the quilt, unless you really want to.

If you can't find either of these brands, go ahead and try some good-quality cotton. Your machine will let you know pretty quickly if it's going to like the cotton in the bobbin for the quilting or not.

EXPERT TIP
“ **Really good machine quilting comes from a combination of practice and using the right materials for your machine. The correct mix of bobbin thread, needle, thread tension, single needle plate, and traction (in the form of gloves, paddles, or Silicon sheets on your machine bed) can make or break your efforts. Experiment until you find the right combination.** ”

Question 157:
What needles should I use?

The needle you use depends on the thread you're working with. Most cotton threads will work fine with a sharps, quilting, or universal needle. For any other type of specialty threads, such as rayon, polyester, or silk, a topstitch needle might work better. A topstitch needle has a longer groove in the back through which the thread travels. Because the groove is designed differently, there is less pulling and snagging on the thread, which means fewer thread breaks.

You absolutely must change the needle frequently. Figure a new needle for every two bobbin changes, more if the thread starts breaking.

Possibly even more important than the right needle for your machine quilting is using a single needle plate on your sewing-machine bed. The needle plate is the metal plate that rests over the feed dogs and bobbin casing. The machine's needle goes down into the machine's bed through a hole in the needle plate, where the bobbin thread is picked up and the stitch loop is formed. Most machines come with a zigzag plate, which has a wider hole to accommodate the different decorative stitches your machine can sew. But you can often buy a single needle plate from the dealer. This plate has a small hole and only allows your needle to go straight up and down in the plate—no side-to-side action here. Because the hole is smaller, there is less push and pull on the fabric as the needle moves through it. Your fabric won't get jammed into the machine's workings.

Question 158:
Can I use invisible thread?

Invisible thread is a good option for quilting that you'd like to be invisible on top of the quilt. It can be used in the bobbin as well. But it's a finicky thread and has its own set of rules for successful sewing.

You will need to use the proper needle for invisible thread. I prefer to use a topstitch needle, either 80/12 or 90/14 size. A topstitch needle has a groove along the back shaft that eases the thread through the needle as it's moving through the fabric. Because of the groove, there usually is less snagging and breaking of your thread. Topstitch needles are suitable for most machine quilting threads, from cottons to rayons and silks. They are a little harder to track down, but your local quilt shop owners should be able to order them for you.

When you're quilting with invisible thread, you will need to slow down your quilting speed. Invisible thread is made from a polyester plastic and as it moves through the fabric, it heats and stretches. By slowing down your stitching speed, there will be less stretching.

You will probably need to loosen the top thread tension. Experiment with your machine's tension settings on your practice quilt sandwich and when your tension looks correct, write down the settings you've discovered on the sandwich.

Finally, if you are using the invisible thread in the bobbin, there are two things you will need to do. First, as you wind the bobbin, gently place your finger on the top of the spinning bobbin to slow the winding process down. This goes back to the issue of the thread stretching when heated and the slow-down will keep the thread cooler. Also, only wind the bobbin halfway. Yes, this will cause you to rewind more often, but it will prevent the thread from stretching.

Question 159:
What is stippling?

Stippling refers to any overall stitching pattern used in machine quilting. The pattern can be wiggles, straight lines, hearts, stars, circles—whatever is repeated throughout the entire quilt. Most machine quilters work on perfecting a small arsenal of stippling stitches for their quilting because stippling serves so many purposes. If you're quilting large areas, large stippling can quickly finish your quilt. You can shrink the size of the stippling to fill in areas of the quilt around more controlled and planned patterns.

RIGHT Stippling is a quilting technique that can be done by hand or machine.

Question 160:
What about stencils and other set quilt patterns?

There are literally thousands of quilt stencils and patterns on the market. Most are useable for both machine and hand quilting. But,

wherever possible, if you're machine quilting, try to find continuous-line stencils. These quilting patterns are designed so that there will be the

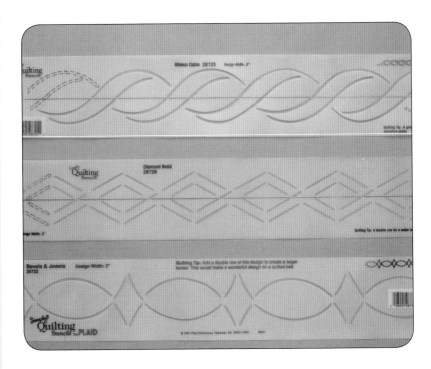

fewest number of starts and stops within the quilting. Because you will probably be able to see the starts and stops, continuous-line patterns help improve the look of the quilting.

Stencil and pattern lines can be transferred onto the quilt's top with erasable marking pens or pencils, chalk, or other marking tools made especially for this task. It's very important that you read the directions for using and removing the marks, and that you test the marking material on similar fabric or scraps from your quilt's construction before using them on your quilt.

ABOVE There are so many different quilt stencils available for purchase that your quilt can have almost any look or feel you wish. From Celtic braids to traditional circle motifs, there is no limit to your quilting designs.

When it's time to quilt, you'll be stitching along these guidelines to create the patterns. Stencils are used mostly for formal or traditional quilting.

Question 161:
What is long-arm quilting?

In recent years, many quilters have set up thriving cottage industries around their long-arm quilting services. A long-arm quilting machine is an industrial-grade machine, usually having only a very fast straight stitch, which works with a large frame designed to support the quilt. The long-arm system may, or may not, include a computer program to aid in the quilting.

Long-armers cater to the quilter who enjoys making the tops but who doesn't want, or is unable, to accomplish the quilting. A quilter will hire a long-armer to complete the quilting for them. This is a good alternative to quilts that are on a deadline or if you haven't learned to machine quilt yet, or if you really don't like to machine quilt.

Most local quilt shops will have long-armers who are known by the shop. The more intricate your quilting, the more you will pay for the service and, be warned, long-armers get very busy with work close to the holiday season. Long-armers can offer custom work where you will have very intricate quilting highlighting individual design elements throughout the quilt, or simple, overall designs that just finish the quilt. The cost will depend on the quilter's skill and the detail involved.

LEFT The HQ Fusion by Handi Quilter shown below is a long-arm quilting machine. It requires a special frame to mount the quilt onto during quilting, and the operator works the machine from above. Long-arm quilting has become a thriving home business for many quilters looking to supplement their hobby or make a living.

N.B. This photo is courtesy of Handi Quilter.

Question 162:
How do I hold the sandwich while I quilt?

The most important technique to master while you machine quilt is manipulating the fabric while it's under your sewing-machine foot. Because the fabric can slip and you can strain your neck and shoulder muscles from exerting too much pressure while you work the quilt under the needle, you should use some sort of traction for handling the quilt, literally.

There are many types of gloves available today that provide a machine quilter with the traction needed to move the quilt sandwich around. These gloves usually have rubber dots, or rubberized fingers on them to grip the fabric. They come in different sizes and different glove materials, but all will help to move the fabric freely. Keep trying different styles until you find what works for you.

If you don't like the gloves, there are also small hand paddles that work in a similar fashion. The weighted paddles are placed in each hand and pressed down on the quilt's top. It's the paddle that moves the sandwich around.

Some quilters prefer to use a

ABOVE The key to good free-motion machine quilting comes in large part from the quilter being able to freely move the sandwich under the needle, at a consistent speed, to achieve evenly spaced stitches.

silicon spray or silicon sheet on their machine's bed to loosen up the quilt sandwich and allow movement.

Whatever is used, the point is that you must be able to move the quilt freely under the needle to successfully machine quilt. Visit your local quilt or fabric shop and explore the different tools made for machine quilting.

Once you've settled on the right tool for manipulating the quilt, you can work its bulk by rolling up the quilt and quilting it in sections or, if you've spray-basted your quilt (which creates an even adhesion of the quilt's layers) you can just bunch it up as you go along. With very large quilts, you'll struggle more to work their bulk under the machine's bed. Since free-motion quilting requires the feed dogs to be dropped on your machine, you may need to turn your quilt and work it from different directions to handle the stitching.

Even with gloves on, it's easy to become distracted while you're stitching and have an accident. Always watch where your hands are while you sew and quilt. Spread your hands out to distribute the pressure on the quilt and keep them away from the needle. Your hands will work the quilt sandwich under the needle. In time and with practice you will become very adept at free-motion quilting.

Question 163:
How do I pull my quilting thread tails out of sight?

When you start machine quilting, lower the needle into the quilt by hand (turning the wheel) and then raise it up. As you raise the needle, the top thread will be looped with the bobbin thread. Make sure your foot is off the machine's pedal so you don't accidentally stitch your fingers! Pull the top thread's tail and you'll see the bobbin thread's loop come up through the same hole that you just stitched. Use your small scissors or a stiletto in the loop and pull the bobbin thread up until you find the tail. Then, holding both the top thread's and the bobbin thread's tails to the side of the needle, take a couple of stitches where they come up. This will secure the threads to the quilt top. Snip the threads to the stitches and start quilting.

When you're done with your quilting, you can repeat this process, or you can leave your thread tails in the quilt's back. If you leave the threads on the back, tie the two threads together to make a secure knot and then use a small needle to weave the tails back into the quilt's middle layer (batting). Master quilters never have loose threads showing on their quilts, front or back.

Question 164:
How do I perfect my machine quilting?

Good machine quilting is all about even stitches, proper thread tension, and smooth corners and curves. These attributes are best learned by practice, but there are measures you can take to help you succeed.

Start by setting up your machine properly. If you're working with straight-line stitching, your feed dogs are up (engaged) and you'll probably use your walking, or even-feed foot on your machine. If you have a single needle plate, put it on and make sure you remember it's there. I put a little note on the front of my machine to remind myself that the single needle plate is in. Use a fresh machine needle that is appropriate for the thread you're using, wind a couple of bobbins and get comfortable. If your machine is not set in flush with your table top and you have an extension table, use it. For straight-line stitching, you'll be following either your markings or lines on the quilt. In general, you'll want to start from the quilt's center and work your way to the outside. This helps prevent the fabric from bunching, puckering, and folding while you stitch. It also helps the quilt to hang flat when it's finished.

If you're working with free-motion quilting, your set-up is similar: single needle plate, fresh needle appropriate for the thread, flush table mount or extension table if possible, and extra wound bobbins.

But, if your feed dogs are down (retracted), you should have a darning or free-motion foot on the machine's shank.

As with straight stitching, you'll want to start in the middle of the quilt and stitch your way out to the edges. Another important point when you're planning your quilting is that you maintain an equal amount of quilting throughout the quilt. In other words, if the center is densely quilted with very little exposed fabric showing, you need to carry that dense quilting to the borders as well. If you're working with an all-over pattern, again make sure you're working evenly throughout the quilt. The reason why is that the quilting itself will "take up" or constrict your quilt sandwich. The more dense the quilting, the more constricted your quilt will be under that stitching. If you have areas of your quilt that are tightly quilted and areas that are loosely quilted with a more open pattern, your quilt will not hang right and it might not even lay right. The quilt will end up buckled and won't look good. Make sure your quilting is balanced throughout the quilt and your finished quilt will look nicer for the extra attention it receives.

It's been said before that practice makes your quilting better over time. So does warming up beforehand. With free-motion quilting, your hands become rhythmic with your machine. Your movements begin to flow and you can find yourself almost hypnotized by your quilting. But it can take a bit to get there.

I suggest you take your practice sandwich (see Question 154) and quilt some simple swirls and squiggles on it to loosen up your muscles and brain. When you're bored with the practice sandwich, you'll be ready to start on your quilt.

One of the attributes to good machine quilting is that your stitches are even. In hand quilting, your stitch count is controlled by your skill with the hand needle. In machine quilting, your stitch count is controlled by the relationship between the speed of the stitching and your pace as you manipulate the sandwich under the needle. You need to learn to work together with your machine to achieve your best stitching. It's far better that you have evenly spaced stitches—no matter how long they are—than to have some big and some small stitches working along the same line. Most beginners to machine quilting are afraid to run their machine too fast. They slow down so they can carefully watch what they are doing with the stitching. But this is actually counterintuitive to how machine quilting works. The faster you sew (how hard you press on your pedal usually), the better flow and control you will have with your quilting. Practice building up your sewing speed. Then, carefully look at your finished stitches. Pay attention to how your speed affected your stitching. You'll start seeing improvements in your stitching as your comfort with speed grows.

17

BINDING

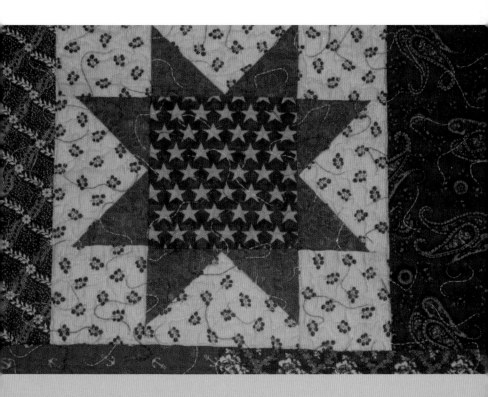

Question 165:
What's the best way to trim the quilt edges to prepare for binding?

This is another one of those quilt moments when I tend to do things a little differently from the norm, but with consistent success. After my quilt is completely quilted, I iron it as flat as possible. If I'm working on a quilt that has embellishments, I'm a little easier about ironing the sections with the embellishments but, in general, I really want to achieve a flat quilt top. Then, using very large cutting mats covering a dining table or other large surface, I spread my quilt top on the cutting surface and trim the edges of the quilt.

To do the trimming I use a combination of a 15-inch square ruler and an 8 1/2 by 24-inch ruler.

Starting from a long side of the quilt, I work from the bottom up. I place the square ruler in the quilt's corner, using the 45-degree line to line up the ruler evenly against the corner. I usually trim all three layers of the quilt to create the crispest line possible. When I have my corner ruler in position, I then use the longer ruler to establish the first cutting line along the border's edge. It's a little instinctive but I try to make an even cut parallel to the first straight seam line I can refer to. If my border is about 6 1/2 inches, I will usually trim it to an even 6 inches using the border's seam line as my guide. You need to make sure your quilt is as flat and straight as

RIGHT Square up your quilt sandwich's corners before binding your quilt.

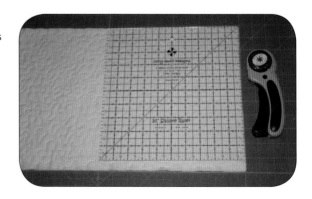

possible for this first cut because it will be used to square up all of the remaining cuts. When your rulers, corner and long, are in place, go ahead and make your cut with the rotary cutter, from the bottom up. If your edges are longer than the ruler, cut three-quarters of the way up the ruler and then nudge it up more, making sure the bottom half of the ruler edge continues to follow the cut you just made exactly. When you get close to the upper corner, use the square ruler to square off the corner, turn the quilt to the next edge and continue with the combination of long-ruler and corner-ruler cuts. In this way, you should end up with the straightest possible quilt edges. If you fold the quilt in half, you should find that you've matched up your corners and edges well.

Question 166:
What are common binding styles?

Bindings are strips of fabric that are wrapped around the quilt's exposed edges, to both protect and finish the quilt. The bindings will suffer a lot of wear and tear between use and washing (unless it's an art quilt that hangs all of the time) and it's important to master making and using a binding for the quilt's long-term survival.

To cover the basics of what's used for bindings, I will say that there are single-fold bindings, double-fold bindings, and edge-turned bindings. There are also specialty finishes for your quilt's edges such as facings, ruffles, and prairie points.

Most quilts are best served by a double-fold binding. These bindings

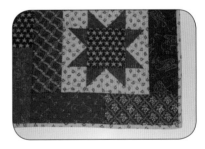

ABOVE Binding can become a design element for your quilt, when it's made in a contrasting color.

are the most durable and protective of the quilt's edges. It's easy to master and simpler to achieve than a single-fold binding. The following instructions only address working with a double-fold binding.

Question 167:
How wide should binding be?

Another question where the answer is completely personal to the quilter. Assuming you're working with a double-fold binding, which is what I use exclusively on my quilts; I work with a 2 ½-inch strip. I fold it in half lengthwise, creating a 1 ¼-inch strip. I sew the binding's open edge along the quilt's edge with a ¼-inch seam allowance and fold it over to the back of the quilt. That leaves me with a ½-inch of binding showing on the quilt front and a ½-inch of binding to tack down on the back. Some quilters prefer a narrower binding to work on the back, but I think it's easier to accurately sew down a wider strip to the back.

Question 168:
What color fabric should I use for binding?

There is no set rule about the color of your binding, but you want to select a color that will blend with the top of the quilt. The binding is a finishing touch for your quilt and, in most cases, it should not take away from the quilt's design. It can even match the outermost border and become a part of the border instead of a separate element.

Of course, if you decide that you want your binding to stand out as a design element for your quilt, there's nothing wrong with that. It can be a very effective and attractive alternative to a binding that fades into the background.

For instance, consider piecing different strips of fabrics together for the binding. This can be done in random lengths to create a scrappy look. Or, for a more graphic, contemporary look, piece regular lengths of alternating colors, (black and white maybe). This will serve as a snazzy frame for your quilt.

Question 169:
How do I make binding?

To make a double-width binding, start by calculating how much fabric you'll need.

First, determine how many strips you will need by adding the inches of your quilt's four sides. A 90-inch square quilt will need 360 inches of binding. Add an additional 12 inches to that number for overage and joining the strips. So you'll need at least 372 inches of binding. Working with the 40-inch width of the fabric, divide 372 by 40 to determine how many strips you'll need. The answer is 9.3, so round that up to ten strips. Then, multiply ten by how wide your strips will be. In this case, it's 2 1/2 inches, which means you'll need 25 inches of fabric cut into ten 2 1/2-inch strips.

Cut your strips from selvage to selvage. To join them, take two strips, right sides together, and face them at a right angle to each other. The front strip will slightly overlap the back strip. Draw a pencil line bisecting the diagonal, pin, and then sew along that line. Trim the seam to 1/4 inch with scissors. Open and press the seam to reduce bulk. Repeat with the next strip and so on until they are all joined together.

When your strips are joined, starting from one end, fold the strip in half lengthwise, wrong sides together and iron. Make sure to match the raw edges accurately. I keep the binding rolled on a piece of cardboard until it's time to use it to keep it from wrinkling.

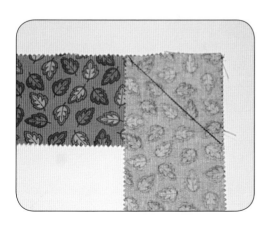

LEFT Join your binding strips by sewing a seam along the right angle. Be accurate, going from corner to corner. When you unfold the strip, you should have the strips joined perfectly.

Question 170:
How do I sew mitered corners?

I think this is a lot of fun. Starting in the center of the quilt's top edge, pin the binding, matching the open edge of the folded binding to the quilt's trimmed edge. Make sure they match exactly. Leave an 8-inch tail and then start sewing the binding to the quilt's edge, using a ¼-inch seam allowance. Pull the pins as you go along. When you reach the corner, stop stitching about a ¼-inch from the corner. Back stitch to secure, clip

threads, and remove the quilt from under the sewing machine.

With the quilt side that you're working on facing up, fold the binding up and away from the quilt's edge at a 45-degree angle. Then, fold the binding back down over itself and onto the next edge of the quilt. Pin the corner in place. Turn the quilt so you're working on the next edge, pin the binding in place along the edge and start sewing again a ¼-inch from the corner (backstitch the corner) with a ¼-inch seam allowance. Continue this for the remaining three corners and edges.

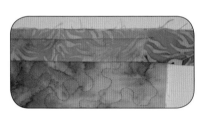

1   Sew a ¼-inch seam from the raw edge of the binding/sandwich and stop a ¼-inch from the end of the side.

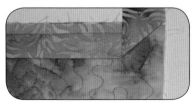

2   Fold the loose end of the strip up at a 45-degree angle and press in place.

3   Fold the loose end of the strip back down over itself and press a crease that matches the edge of the sandwich. Continue sewing a ¼-inch seam from the raw edge until you reach the next side's end.

Question 171:
How do I join the binding ends?

About 8 inches from the binding ends, stop sewing. Unfold the binding, take the two tails and overlap them until they are in line with the quilt's edge. Trim them so there is a ¼-inch from each tail. Sew a seam to join the two tails and trim the seam. Press open the seam and refold the binding. Pin it in place and finish sewing. Your binding is now attached to the quilt.

1   Join the binding's two tails by sewing them together.

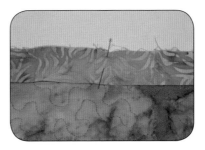

2   Refold the binding, pin in place and finish sewing.

Question 172:
How do I tack binding in place?

Once the binding is in place, bring the quilt to the ironing board, front/top up. Iron the binding up (off of the quilt). Make sure this seam that you're ironing is very crisp and has no hidden folds. Flip the quilt over and then carefully fold and press the binding, wrapping the quilt's edge as you go. One of the factors that distinguishes a great quilt is that the binding completely covers the edge and has no air pockets or empty space under the fold. Most quilters don't iron their bindings, but

I do and have never had a problem with it. It also allows me to get away without pinning or clipping the binding in place while I tack it down to the back. You especially want to iron out the mitered corners. The mitering creates a pocket of sorts, which you can neatly fold into a perfect 45-degree diagonal and press into place.

To hand tack binding, you'll use a blind stitch. Hold the quilt on your lap with the bound edge closest to you. You're looking at the binding. With the hand needle you're most comfortable with and a 20-inch length of thread with a quilter's knot in the end, come up on your first stitch through the front of the binding. Go back into the backing layer and travel the needle just

under the backing to the left (right, if you're left-handed) for about a ¼ inch, then bring the needle up through the backing and the edge of the binding. Come back down again into the backing layer just above the edge where you came out and travel the needle through to the left again for the next stitch. Continue until you're done.

When you come to the mitered corners, you might need to take a couple of tiny stitches along the diagonal fold to hold the fold in place.

I happen to love sewing the binding. I can bring my finished quilt with me to different sit-around events and show it off while I finish working on it. It's also great couch work in front of the television.

1   Your tacking stitches should be about a ¼ inch apart and be nearly invisible.

2   Don't forget to tack down the mitered corners. This makes for a professional finish on the corners.

Question 173:
How can I bind a curved edge?

The binding technique I provided in Question 172 is solely for straight edges. Some quilts have scallops or other rounded curves. Because of this you must prepare your binding strips from bias cut strips. These are strips cut across the diagonal of the fabric's grain. You'll need more fabric for these cuts, but bias strips have a natural tendency to curve and stretch and this allows the curves to be nicely wrapped without pleating or warping.

Start with a perfect square of fabric and cut it in half diagonally at a 45-degree angle. Then, starting at the long edge of one triangle, cut 2 ½-inch strips until you can't cut anymore. Repeat with the other triangle.

To calculate how big a square you will need for the bias strips, take the size of the square, divide by the width of the strip and then multiply by the size of the square. That number is the approximate length in inches of your final bias strip.

So, if you start with a 20-inch square, divide that by 2 ½ (for the strip's width) and you get 8. Multiply 8 by 20 (for the square's inches) and you'll yield about 160 inches of strip.

Piece the strips together the same as you did the straight binding, whether on a curved or straight edge, except in the case of inside points. Scalloped borders create inside points. To join the binding to the points, sew the binding exactly to the middle of the point. Stop stitching and clip the threads. Then, turn the binding at an angle to match the next section of the quilt's edge. This will create a small bunch of fabric at the point behind your needle, but you want this.

When you're done with the stitching and it's time to work the binding to the back of the quilt for tacking, you'll tuck the corners neatly, similar to the right-angle miter corners (see Question 170), and sew into place.

18

FINISHING TOUCHES

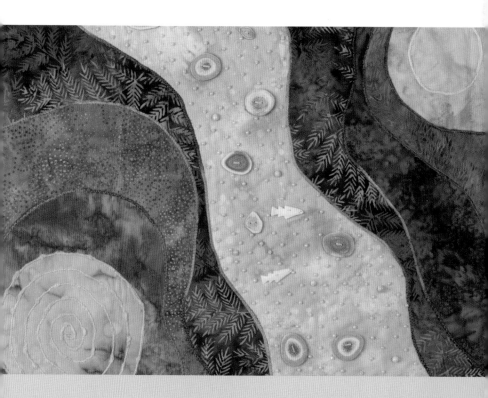

Question 174:
What about embellishments?

There are so many ways to add flair and depth to quilts today, it's become a sub-genre of the craft known as surface design or mixed media. Quilts provide a fabulous canvas for playing with all sorts of embellishments.

Traditional embellishments include buttons, threads, beads, and ribbons. But thinking outside of the box brings in crystals (heat-set crystals that work with a special iron wand are all the rage right now); Angelina fibers, which melt and fuse into the quilt's top creating shine and glitter; yarns; rickrack; paints

of all kinds used to enhance and distinguish designs; rubber stamps with ink made for fabric; scrapbook doo-dads; trinkets, jewelry; found objects; hardware; seashells; photographs; and pretty much anything else that comes to mind.

Embellishments can be sewn, glued, melted, impressed, and painted. When you are applying embellishments that have any weight to them (metal coins, heavy buttons, etc.) be mindful of the way the embellishment might distort the quilt's surface. If you're working with heavy items, you can reinforce the

BELOW Mrs. Froggy's Dowry by Jake Finch features beads of all sizes and shapes, as well as glass charms. The beads make the quilt sparkle.

Flowing Between Dusk and Dawn by Jake Finch also has beads, but these beads are more subtle. Also, handmade buttons from antlers and ivory add to the rustic feel of the quilt.

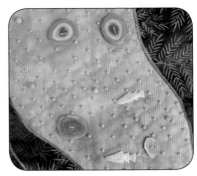

back of the quilt's top with fusible interfacing, which will help support the item's weight. Of course, this is done before the quilt is assembled, so you'll have to plan around it for the quilting and other work on the quilt.

With the explosion of art quilting over the last decade, quilt artists are providing lots of written materials—magazines, articles, books, blogs—to spread the news on how they accomplish their designs. Internet searches for instructions will yield many references, most for free, on how to embellish quilts.

Question 175:
What's the best way to add beads to my quilts?

Beads add a wonderful blast of bling to your quilts. They come in all shapes and sizes and many a quilter has discovered a new addiction from a simple trip to a local bead store. It's also easy to become overwhelmed, so when you're starting on the beaded path, focus on one need and work around that. For instance, if you're on the prowl for purple beads, you can narrow your focus enough to only look for purple. This makes it a lot simpler than facing 40,000 varieties of beads and having to make a decision.

Beads are best sewn to your quilt. Seed beads and bugle beads (long, tube-like beads) are very tiny and you'll need to make a small investment in bead thread. Nymo is one brand of beading thread that is especially strong. You can also use quilting thread, which is heavier than standard cotton thread. Try to work with a color that will either blend into the bead's color or the quilt itself. As far as needles go, turn to your hand piecing and quilting needles (the small betweens and sharps). They will probably be thin enough to pass through the seed beads and they are sturdier than the beading needles, which are so thin they can bend and break while you're working. If the betweens and sharps don't work, by all means use the beading needles.

The next question you'll need to answer is if you're going to quilt around the beadwork or add the beadwork after the quilting is completed? Whenever possible,

I advise that you do your beading after the top has been completely assembled, quilted and bound but before you add the sleeve and label. With a clean back, you'll be able to stitch your beads down and bury the threads in the middle layer of the quilt. Also, the stitching to hold the beads in place serves as additional quilting for the quilt. It's a lot easier than having to work the quilting around the beading.

But, for certain projects you may need to add the beads first. In this case, make sure you've reinforced any areas that will handle extra weight from the beads and embellishments with interfacing. Also, if you're machine quilting the piece, make sure your sewing machine's parts will have enough clearance around the beads so you're not hitting them with your needle.

When you attach a bead to the quilt, work with a length of thread about 15 to 20 inches long. Make a quilter's knot at the end, leaving about a 2-inch tail below the knot. Come up through the back of the quilt (or the top if your quilt isn't yet assembled) and pick up a bead on the front. Bring the bead to the quilt surface then place a stitch down into the quilt right at the bead's edge. Come up again next to the last stitch, pick up another bead and repeat until you have several beads on the chain. To end the chain, come up in the back of the last bead added, thread your needle through that bead and pull the needle down through the top right in front of the bead for a second time. Knot the thread on the quilt's back and snip, leaving a couple of inches for the tail. You can go back and feed both the start tail and the end tail into the quilt's middle to hide the threads when you're done with the project.

RIGHT
Embellishments should enhance your quilt's existing design.

Question 176:
How can I use photos in my quilts?

Over the last ten years, with the explosion of digital photography, scrapbooking, and photo-transfer techniques, it has become incredibly easy for quilters to incorporate photographs into their work. There are many books on the market about working with photographs and quilts, but I can offer enough to get you started.

Photos can be printed directly onto fabric sheets that are then incorporated into the quilt. Photos can also be printed onto special papers that, when ironed onto fabric, will transfer the image. In this case, you'll be working with a reverse image unless you're photo-tech savvy enough to reverse the image beforehand on your computer. The printing for these techniques

happens either with an ink-jet printer (color or black and white) or a photo copier. Laser-jet printer ink is not suitable for the chemicals used in these transfer mediums.

The fabric sheets on the market are treated with special chemicals that retain the printer's inks. You can also make your own transfer sheets, a process that's involved, but probably much less expensive in the long run. If you're working with commercial sheets, know that some brands have you soak the sheets after the printing is completed to "set" the inks. Some brands don't require this step.

I use Printed Treasures and the transfer sheets by The Electric Quilt Co., the same makers of quilt design software. Neither of these sheets

RIGHT *Fidget Quilt*, 2007, by Jake Finch uses photographs and printed quotes to enhance a quilt that will be used by someone with brain impairment, such as a dementia patient.

have to be washed after printing.

The fabric sheets are available in several different fabrics and weights, including silk, cotton, cotton lawn, canvas, and cotton duck. I also printed my quilt labels onto these sheets and I can attest that my printed labels have survived numerous washings whereas my fabric pen-written labels have not.

Question 177:
What are quilt labels?

A quilt label is usually found on the back of a quilt and offers information about who made the quilt, when, where, and why. It's probably made from a separate piece of fabric and can either be written on with a permanent fabric pen (Micron is one brand commonly used among quilters), or printed onto pre-treated fabric sheets with a computer printer.

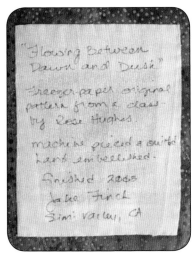

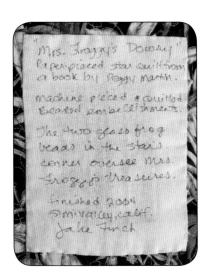

LEFT AND ABOVE Some quilters argue that a label is the most important part of the quilt. Knowing who made it, when, and why helps with appraisals, tracking down lost owners, and establishing the quilt's history. Labels are also the best way to make your quilt personal for its recipient.

Question 178:
Why do I have to bother with a quilt label?

Think about all of the antique quilts found in attics and at flea markets that have no label. These discoveries are treasure troves of history, but the makers remain anonymous. A label gives the maker stature. It also helps quilt historians and quilt buffs learn about the maker's culture. Labels are invaluable in ascertaining a quilt's age and its roots. The information provided on a label can actually elevate the value of a quilt.

In the case of contemporary quilts, a label provides a way for a lost or stolen quilt to find its way home. If you submit your quilts to shows, a label is mandatory as the show's organizers are sometimes handling thousands of quilts. The last thing you will want to happen after spending weeks, months, or years creating your quilt is for it to be lost.

Question 179:
What should be included on a label?

A label needs to have:
- Quilt title
- Maker's name
- Quilter's name (if different from the maker)
- Address or at least city/state/country
- Phone number
- Date(s) made
- If the quilt was made from a pattern, which one? This is helpful, especially when someone falls in love with the pattern and wants to track it down. It's also a nice gesture to give credit to the designer.
- The story behind the quilt: New techniques, why it was made, interesting fabrics, or anything else that makes the quilt unique.
- If the quilt is given to someone else, who is the recipient and why?
- Some quilters include washing instructions on the quilt.
- You can even include jokes, quotes, stories or anything else that makes the quilt personal to the recipient.

Question 180:
How do I attach the label to the quilt?

It's easy enough to say just stitch the label to the back of the quilt and be done with it, but there are enough instances of labels being removed by someone trying to steal the quilt from a show or other venue that you should want that label to be very secure. Here's the next-to-impossible-to-remove method for attaching your label to your quilt.

Make the label in any method you wish—by hand writing, printed onto fabric printer sheets, or even machine embroidered—and then finish the edges. Turning the edges under will work fine.

Then, put fusible webbing to the back (wrong) side of the label and iron the label onto the quilt's back. Labels are usually located in the lower left corner on the back of the quilt. When the label is adhered to the backing, slip-stitch the label's edges to the quilt back. This should be enough to keep it in place. For an added measure, you can add the label to the quilt back before you quilt the quilt. The quilting itself will provide extra security for the label, but you may not want the stitching to run through the label's writing.

One more technique that I use for additional security and recognition of my quilts is I machine quilt my signature into the quilt's border or edge. I write my name in cursive/script along the edge and then sew along the writing several times until it my name is clearly seen. Use a free-motion foot and drop your feed dogs to do this, just as you would with machine quilting.

Question 181:
What is a sleeve and how do I make one?

A sleeve is a fabric tube sewn to the top edge of the quilt back to hold a hanging rod. Most sleeves for shows are required to be 4 inches in depth to accommodate the variety of tools used to hang quilts. To make a sleeve, measure the quilt's width at the top edge and cut a piece of fabric that length by 9 inches wide. Fold the fabric along the length in half, right sides together, and stitch ¼ inch along the open edges. Turn the tube right side out and press. You should now have a strip of fabric 4 ½ inches by the length of the quilt's top edge. Fold under each

end of the strip by a ½ inch, press and sew in place. Then slip stitch the top and bottom edges of the sleeve onto the quilt's back, about 2 inches from the quilt's top, making sure the sleeve is very straight. Leave ½ inch of play in the tube so a rod will not protude out of the front when the quilt is hung up.

RIGHT
A sleeve is easy to add to a quilt's back and allows the quilt to be hung without stretching or pulling.

Question 182:
How do I wash my quilt?

Assuming we're not talking about antique or art quilts, you can wash your quilts in a washing machine with cold water using a delicate detergent and dry them in a dryer on a delicate setting. There are

detergents on the market that are made for quilts. You can also wash the quilt by hand, again with cold water and a delicate detergent. Over the course of the quilt's life, it will soften with age, handling, and washing. Most quilters prize the effect that repeated washing has on the quilt, making it soft and supple. Also, some battings will continue shrinking slightly with the first couple of washings and it will create a more crinkly appearance in your quilts.

When you're handling an antique quilt, washing may not be an option. Dyes used decades and centuries ago may run and some fabric may be worn to the point of imminent destruction. You might be able to spot-clean some areas.

You can gently vacuum an old quilt to remove the dirt. For some quilts, this could be your only safe option. If you can, spread the quilt on a bed. Use a hand attachment covered with pantyhose or cheesecloth and a layer of tulle—

the netting fabric used in ballet skirts—or screen from the hardware store. Lay the tulle or screen on top of the quilt and vacuum through it, using an up-and-down motion, not side-to-side. The screening/tulle helps prevent the quilt from getting sucked up into the vacuum.

Dry cleaning is an option for wool and silk quilts, but only as a last-ditch effort. The chemicals can be very harsh on delicate fibers, so don't rush to the dry cleaner unless you must. See if you can find a cleaner who works with bridal gowns and other specialty items. You need to make sure the best care is given to your quilt, especially if it's an antique. Ask that they don't mark the quilt in any way and do not use safety pins on the quilt itself.

Question 183:
How should I store my quilts?

Quilts can be stored in cabinets, trunks, hung on walls, stacked on quilt racks, draped over furniture, or tucked onto beds. Some quilters use pillowcases for long-term quilt storage. Most quilts fold up nicely to fit into a pillowcase. You can also purchase acid-free tissue paper and archival-quality boxes for folding quilts, which is an excellent

way to wrap and store fragile, antique quilts. If you're storing or displaying quilts in an area that receives direct, unfiltered sunlight, be sure to rotate your quilts every three months. Consider coating windows with UV filters so the sun won't fade your quilt's colors. Also, never permanently store quilts in plastic, whether bags or boxes. It's too easy for moisture to become trapped with the quilts, and mildew is almost impossible to remove from quilts. If your quilts are folded up and stashed somewhere, you do want to open, re-fold and use them periodically. Over time, the folds can become a unwanted permanent feature of your quilt, not to mention that the lack of air circulation for the fabric is not good. Folding on the bias reduces the likelihood of permanent creases.

Another option for storing quilts, besides folding, is to roll your quilts. I've seen some quilts rolled onto old wrapping paper rolls with tissue paper covering the outside. Don't roll quilts with embellishments or old quilts.

Question 184:
How do I safely display my quilts?

Quilt racks and decorative ladders are excellent ways to display quilts. Quilts can be safely folded and displayed for all to enjoy.

There are also special trunks and cases made from clear plastic or glass that can house and show off your quilts.

Most quilts can be safely hung on walls for display. If the quilt has a sleeve, a dowel can be inserted through the sleeve and the dowel can then rest on curtain-rod hooks or decorative grips. A slat can also be inserted through the sleeve and then mounted to the wall. If a quilt doesn't have a sleeve and you don't want to add one, binder clips or hangers can hold the quilt up by hooks or pushpins. Small quilts can even be professionally framed behind glass or plexiglass.

Some quilters create vignettes for their quilts. A small collection of baby quilts can be displayed in antique cribs and bassinets. Wall quilts with a related theme or color can be hung together on walls.

ABOVE Show off your hard work by displaying your quilt on a wall.

19

IMPROVING YOUR SKILLS

Question 185:
What makes a great quilt?

A great quilt features excellent technique, balanced composition, creative use of fabrics and color, and that added spark of imagination that makes the viewer say, "Wow!"

As an impassioned quilter, you need to learn about all of these aspects of what makes a great quilt in whatever discipline you choose, because it will enhance your experience overall. But, you don't need to learn everything today. Each project you undertake will add to your arsenal of quilt tools and skills and each should be enjoyed for its own merit and process. This is supposed to be fun.

Still, it never hurts to look at what other people consider to be great quilts. Visit those bigger shows and really look at the prize winners, and those that didn't win but are still hanging. Can you tell what that maker did well enough to land her quilt in a show? What inspiration can you get from other people's quilts?

Question 186:
Why should I always keep my first quilt?

Years from now, when you're a firmly entrenched quilt addict, you'll appreciate looking back on your first effort and evaluating your growth as a quilter. You'll also become an inspiration for all of those new quilters who will follow in your stitching steps. Keep your first project. Worship its baby steps. And don't let the dog anywhere near it!

NEXT PAGE *The Beast* was my first quilt and I treasure it for so many reasons, not the least of which is being able to see how far I've come! Try to keep your first project. There will be so many more you can give away.

Question 187:
Why should I connect with other quilters?

While the actual act of quiltmaking is generally a solitary act (quilting bees aside), being part of a community of quilters, however small or large, provides a wonderful opportunity for growth and friendship. Quilters are a happy, joyful bunch of people who love their fabrics. Since there are all kinds of quilting out there to enjoy, from hand appliqué to contemporary piecing and more, there's a lot to share with others.

The easiest way to find more quilters is to join a quilt guild (called quilt bee in some areas). A guild is a group of people coming together to explore a shared interest more deeply. Most modern guilds don't have admission requirements, though there are a few that ask you to prove your skills to them. These are the exceptions, not the norm. The best way to track down a guild in your area is to visit a quilt show, which is probably hosted by the local guild, or to ask at your local quilt shops.

You can also try an Internet search for quilt guilds in your area and surrounding towns.

Question 188:
Why should I support my local quilt shop?

ABOVE Cotton & Chocolate Quilt Company, in Thousand Oaks, California.

Big fabric retailers have their role in the quilt industry and it's nothing to take for granted. Many regions can't support a local quilt shop. If you're lucky enough to live in an area with a quilt shop, though, your resources for the quilt life have just increased greatly.

Your local quilt shop is a direct link to your love of quilts. Many are owned and operated by quilters who wanted to spend more time around their passion. Most are mom-and-pop shops whose staff will, and should, bend over backwards for your business.

Your local shop can provide on-site technique tutoring and help in selecting fabrics. Shops often offer classes and workshops. You can network with other quilters. Special orders for fabric and supplies should never be a problem. And you should feel as if you're part of a bigger community, because you are.

A great shop makes you feel welcome, never sneers at your questions, and instills a sense of fun and joy for quilting. You should almost feel like you're home when you're in a great shop, which is why you should support your local shop, whenever possible.

Question 189:
Why should I keep a quilt journal?

Maintaining a quilt journal reminds you of your accomplishments and it's an important and fun way to reinforce your love of quilts. A simple scrapbook or binder is perfect for this job.

Your journal should have one or more photographs of the quilts you've made, whether you've kept them or not; along with the date made; the reason it was made; any special techniques or materials used; and any other memories that went along with it. Your journal also serves as a resumé of your work, backs up insurance claims (this is a good place to keep appraisal copies if you have any, see Question 191), and provides your family with a guide into your work.

If you collect quilts, you should also include those in your journal. Track the information on where and how you acquired the quilt, the cost, the condition, and any information you may have been told.

Question 190:
What's the best way to photograph my quilts?

There can be many reasons why you will need to photograph your quilt, from submitting a quilt into a show to verifying insurance information to updating your quilt journal. Knowing some basics will enable you to get the best shots without having to hire a professional photographer.

First, know that quilts really are three-dimensional. The quilt stitching provides depth and texture to the quilt and the best quilt photos show that depth.

You will need an area in which you can either hang the quilt fully or lay it out completely. Whether you're working indoors or outdoors, being able to see the entire quilt is necessary. You will also need to be able to position the camera so that it is perfectly parallel to the quilt. If the camera is tilted even slightly as the shot is taken, it can distort the quilt's appearance. A tripod or other steady, level surface is best to work with to keep your camera steady.

If you're outdoors, wait until the sky is overcast. Direct sunlight can wash out your quilt's colors. Turn off your flash. If you're laying the quilt on the ground, make sure it's stretched out well. To take the shot from above, position the quilt under a balcony or ladder that you can look down from. Take many shots from several angles. Don't forget the close-ups either. Many shows require a detail shot as well as an overall shot. Working with a digital camera will allow you to make sure you're framing the shot well.

If indoors is your choice, watch how the natural light filters through the windows. Large sliding glass doors can offer excellent lighting. Again, try to not use the flash. If you can hang your quilt and frame it entirely, this will help get a great shot. If there's a large, batting-covered design wall, your quilt should be able to stick to it. If there's not enough light provided by the windows, turn on the lights in the room. If you're able to, position all of the lights from the same side of the quilt. This will emphasize the stitching's texture.

Question 191:
Do I need to have my quilt appraised?

Sometimes. An appraisal is a written evaluation of your quilt's value. It can be used for insurance purposes or to determine a sale price of a quilt.

There are certified quilt appraisers available throughout the United States. Some specialize in antique quilts, others in art quilts, and still others in contemporary quilts. A certified appraiser has gone through rigorous coursework and a training period for quilt appraisals.

Currently, the American Quilter's Society is the largest organization to provide certifications for appraisers. Its website (www.americanquilter.com) offers a list of appraisers working through its program.

Often, quilt appraisers are found at quilt shows. They can sometimes provide written appraisals on-site or follow up with an in-depth appraisal that might be needed for insurance purposes.

Question 192:
Should my quilts be insured?

You need to know that your homeowner's insurance policy will probably NOT cover your quilts in the event of loss or substantial damage. Even if the policy does cover something with a lost or damaged quilt, it might only cover the replacement value of the materials, not the intrinsic or artistic value.

Check with your insurance agent about special endorsements that would cover your quilts. Also, there are a couple of agencies that underwrite quilts. The easiest way to track these down is to search "quilt insurance" on the Internet.

You should also know that quilts may not be insured by shipping companies if they are lost in transit. While you might have purchased added insurance for your quilt when you shipped it off, many carriers won't consider the quilt anything other than a blanket. Make sure that whatever added insurance you purchase through your homeowner's policy or additional quilt insurance policy covers quilts lost in shipment as well.

Question 193:
Are there classes out there for me?

Absolutely! There are classes for every skill level and every interest.

The first place to look for classes is at your local quilt shops and major fabric retailers. Most offer classes and should also have samples of the class project for you to see in advance. Class fees are based on the area in which you're taking a class, the caliber/notoriety of the teacher, the length of the class, and what the class is about.

Beginner's classes are usually given in a series to teach several skills involved with making quilts. But you can easily find classes in specific skills such as quilting your quilt, hand appliqué, and borders.

Other venues for quilt classes are adult-education schools, senior centers, and parks and recreation districts. Many times, ongoing classes for quilting are an integral part of these community programs.

The local quilt guild may also hold workshops that might be open to the public, if you don't want to join the guild.

You might also consider a private teacher if there is something specific you'd like to learn or if you're working through a special project and would like some guidance along the way. Teachers can be tracked down through any of the above venues.

Lastly, quilt shows often offer a full complement of classes for show visitors. The bigger the show, the more classes are offered. These tend to fill up fast, so when you know of a show in your area, book your classes early.

Question 194:
What do I need to take to class with me?

Every quilt class will have a supply list to help you prepare ahead of time. Most general quilt classes—those focusing on techniques and patterns—will require your sewing machine, accessories, and guide book (this is important in case the teacher needs to make adjustments to your machine); scissors and rotary cutter; thread and bobbins; pins; marking pens/pencils; and extra machine needles and hand needles.

To make your classroom experience the best possible, consider bringing a portable daytime light as well as a water bottle. Some quilters also bring chair cushions.

Make sure that you read through the supply list completely at least a week before the class. It is frustrating for the student and disruptive for the class when you do not have all of your supplies with you, and even if you're taking a class in a shop, they might not have what you need on hand.

As far as fabric selection goes for your class project, even if you're stuck, try bringing some fabric with you. A good teacher will help you select more fabrics if you need the help.

The last thing to bring with you to class is your sense of fun, your manners, and your creativity.

Learning more about quilting should be fun and you'll get to spend time with other quilters. Enjoy yourself, but make sure you allow the teacher to do his or her job too.

Question 195:
Should I submit my work to quilt shows?

The short answer is, "Yes!"

Entering a quilt in a show, especially a judged or juried show, can be extremely nerve-wracking. You can feel vulnerable and exposed by the quality of your work. Still, the benefits can be tremendous.

Participating in a quilt show is a fantastic way to step into a new part of the quilt world. Many shows are judged by professional quilters with years of experience behind them. They often evaluate the show's entrants in writing, leaving you with a critique of your work. Beside this feedback, by exposing your skills to those interested in quilters, you can help to inspire others to the cloth.

Question 196:
What's a quilt show like?

If quilters had their own form of a Roman orgy, it would be found at a quilt show!

Quilt shows feature quilts, of course, and there are tons of quilts to be seen. But the larger shows also offer classes, and the larger the show, the better known the teachers are. At a mid- to large-sized show, you'll have the opportunity to learn new techniques and projects from some of the best quilters in the industry, a treat that's well worth your time and money.

Another feature of quilt shows is the vendors who sell there. Think of a quilt show as a quilting mall, where sellers from all over the area come to present their shop's wares to you. If you live in a remote area

ABOVE Picture of the vender area at an International Quilt Festival in Houston.

with few quilt resources, you can often accomplish your year's worth of shopping at one show. Also, and especially at the larger shows, you'll have access to quilt shops from far away. At a large California show last year, retailers from Minnesota, Maine, and Florida were present offering their goods.

Vendors at shows often offer show specials. For instance, you might be able to buy that sewing machine you've been dying for at a discount. Often these machines are set up as demonstration models for the show. After three days of mild use, the shop owner can't resell the machine as new so you could get a discount on the show model.

When you visit a quilt show, there are a couple of things you can do to prepare beforehand to maximize your enjoyment. First, dress comfortably from head to toe. Shows can be crowded affairs and the larger shows present many opportunities for walking. Carry only what you need. A small hanging wallet for credit cards, cash, identification, cell phone, lipstick, and a small snack makes the most sense. Also, carry a small camera with you. You may not be allowed to use the flash, and sometimes there are quilts or exhibits you won't be able to shoot, but for what you can shoot, having a visual record of what you've seen can be very inspiring for your own work. Also, don't take pictures of quilts in the vendors' booths without first asking permission. Some vendors are also the designers and they worry about copyright infringement. Lastly, find out where the restrooms and the food areas are when you get there. Both places are notorious for long lines at quilt shows.

Question 197:
What are quilt challenges?

A quilt challenge is a contest issued to quilters to make a quilt using set guidelines that direct the design.

For instance, the Hoffman Challenge has been around for more than 25 years. Started by Hoffman Fabrics of California, it was initiated by two quilters as a way to sell what they considered to be "ugly" fabrics. By offering prizes to other quilters for their creations with these fabrics, quilters found that they could stretch their creativity through the imposed restrictions on their designs.

Challenges could involve a theme, fabric, technique, color, or any other design variations. By participating in a challenge, a quilter can find herself joyfully extended by her imagination.

ABOVE One of the many quilts made with Hoffman Fabrics Co. annual Hoffman Challenge fabric.

Question 198:
Can children learn to quilt?

Children are wonderful, enthusiastic quilt students. From "driving" the sewing machine to learning basic geometry skills, quiltmaking offers many lessons for children, as well as a fabulous creative outlet.

Many books are on the market that explore how to involve children in quilting, either as individuals being taught at home, or in classroom settings. Children as young as three or four can start coloring and drawing pictures onto fabric squares with fabric markers. Many five-year-olds have the dexterity needed to handle a needle and thread. Rotary cutters probably shouldn't be used by children under eleven or twelve, and only when watched very carefully by an adult. Same with the iron. But children can handle the sewing machine with proper guidance. (You want to watch their little fingers near the needle on this one!)

Many quilt guilds have junior members and/or allow kids to submit their quilts into the guild's shows. Quilt shops often host quilt camps in summer and during school vacations for kids. Scout troops offer badges and other recognition for quilting efforts. Think about enlisting the children in your life in a charity effort involving other kids, like making baby quilts for newborns in the neonatal intensive care unit, or for children who are sick in the hospital.

Consider bringing a child to your local quilt shop to help you select fabric. Most will be immediately drawn to the colors and patterns and it's fun to see what THEY like.

LEFT Children can have a lot of fun learning how to quilt.

Question 199:
How does the Internet help quilters?

The Internet is a wonderful resource for quilters! If you haven't jumped into the quilting cyber-life, you should.

On the Internet, a quilter will find: fabric; books; patterns (including many free patterns); online quilt communities; chats; instructional videos (again, many are free); places to sell your quilts (think www.Etsy.com); quilt history; information on quilt-related travel to museums, special exhibits, and tours; quilt show locators; quilt shop locators; guilds (online and real-time); other quilters; notions; sewing machine retailers; and so much more.

Facebook is becoming a wonderful haven for quilters. With it, you can follow your favorite quilting celebrities (national teachers and designers) and bond with other quilt fanatics.

There are sites to find your lost quilts, sites to locate that fabric you ran out of, and sites to learn a new technique.

Probably one of the most interesting aspects of cyber quilting is the blog. There are hundreds, if not thousands, of people blogging about quilting and related crafts and hobbies. A blog is a type of online journal where people can write about anything that interests them, post pictures and videos. Readers can comment on what is written and conversations abound. There are many, many quilting bloggers and some provide high-quality content, tutorials, and even free patterns and projects to their readers.

There is no reason for today's quilter to be in the closet, working on his or her projects alone, with no input or support from other quilters. It's just too easy to meet other quilters, find what you need, and make new discoveries using the Internet.

Question 200:
What are some organizations out there to support my quilting?

There are many fabulous groups dedicated to quilters. Whatever your niche interest is in the quilt world, there's a group out there to support you.

Many larger shows and contests will require you to join their overriding organization in order to participate. This is not a hardship. Most of these groups provide magazines or catalogues of quilts in their contests and this alone is a wonderful encouragement for your own quilting efforts.

• **International Quilt Association (IQA):**
Overriding organization judging quilts for the Quilts Inc. shows (Think Houston International Quilt Festival among others).
www.quilts.org

• **National Quilting Association (NQA):**
NQA also hosts its own show, and provides quilt teaching, appraising and judging certifications through its group.
www.nqaquilts.org

• **Studio Arts Quilt Associates (SAQA):**
Dedicated to supporting the art quilter, SAQA has a very active membership.
www.saqa.com

• **American Quilter's Society (AQS):** This is the company that produces the Paducah, Kentucky quilt show, among others. It has a close affiliation with the National Quilt Museum, which houses an impressive collection of the past Best of Show winners from the Paducah show, among other quilts in its permanent collection.
www.americanquilter.com
www.quiltmuseum.org

• **Alliance for American Quilts**
This groups works to preserve American quilt history by cataloguing quilts, maintaining a free database of quilts, and by the Save Our Stories (S.O.S.) project where audio interviews with leading quilters are created and maintained for everyone to listen to.
www.allianceforamericanquilts.org

• **International Quilt Study Center:**
Located at the University of Nebraska-Lincoln, the Study Center is dedicated to collecting, preserving, studying, exhibiting, and promoting quilting. It offers graduate studies programs in textile-related studies, both distance and oncampus. It also maintains a free database of articles, videos, and other quilt-related academic research.
www.quiltstudy.org

• **The Quilters' Guild of the British Isles:**
An independent charity dedicated to preserving the heritage and craft of quilting in the UK.
www.quiltersguild.org.uk

• **Quilt Museum and Gallery, York, (UK):**
The Museum holds a unique collection of quilts and related artifacts from around the British Isles dating from the earliest piece in the collection the 1718 Silk Patchwork Coverlet.
www.quiltmuseum.org.uk

• **Twisted Thread:**
A company that organizes textile events across the UK, such as The Festival of Quilts, which is the largest quilting event in Europe.
www.twistedthread.com

• **The London Quilters:**
A London based quilt group that holds monthy meetings and organize occasional quilting exhibitions.
www.londonquilters.org

Of course, this list is not exhaustive. But the major ones are here and can get you started in the wide world of quilting.

Useful Info:
What are the parts of a quilt?

A quilt has three basic parts: the top, batting (middle layer), and backing. The top is the pieced portion of the quilt, the part that's shown off. Batting can be made from cotton, wool, silk, bamboo, recycled soda bottles, polyester, or any combination of these. Different battings are used for different techniques and to achieve a variety of effects for the finished quilt.

The backing can be a solid piece of muslin or a complementary print. It also can serve as another canvas for the quilt's overall design, depending on how much work is desired.

The picture below illustrates the basic parts of a patchwork quilt. A glossary of additional terms can be found at Question 30 (page 38.)

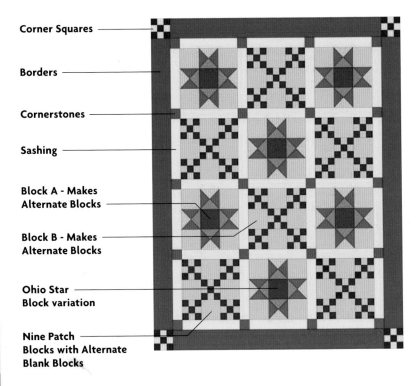

Corner Squares

Borders

Cornerstones

Sashing

Block A - Makes Alternate Blocks

Block B - Makes Alternate Blocks

Ohio Star Block variation

Nine Patch Blocks with Alternate Blank Blocks

Below is a list of great quilting websites:

- **www.batiksplus.com** Looking for a batik? Look no further than this online shop. It prides itself on carrying almost all of the Hoffman batiks, retired and current, and commissions its own designs.
- **www.quiltbooksusa.com** If you're looking for a quilt book or pattern, start here. Period.
- **www.sewthankful.com** Tracy's online shop features the more unusual patterns—wearables and art quilt—along with many great threads.
- **www.nancysnotions.com** If you're into tools and notions, Nancy's has it.
- **www.dharmatrading.com** From dyes to paints, transfer chemicals and ready-for-dye silks and cottons, Dharma offers all of the blank canvas for your quilt masterpiece.
- **www.superiorthreads.com** You can buy some of the very best threads on the market, and scour the site for tips to solve your thread problems.
- **www.ctpub.com** One of the quilting industry's leading book publishers, C&T's site offers links to authors, free patterns and projects, and a free list of lesson plans to teach classes from most of its books. It's why C&T is listed and its competitors are not.
- **www.quilterscache.com** Filled with tons of free patterns and quilting lessons, Quilter's Cache is a good spot to expand your basic skills.
- **www.quilting.about.com** Under founder Janet Wickell's longtime leadership, this website provides a regular free newsletter, quilting instruction and free patterns and books.
- **www.quilts.com** The home site of Quilts, Inc. (think Houston International Quilt Festival), providing show and contest information on the big shows.
- **www.womenfolk.com** Here you'll find articles on quilt history, collected or written by Judy Anne Breneman. There are free patterns as well.
- **www.americanquiltstudygroup.org** This non-profit group supports the study of quilting in America. You'll find scholarships and grant offers and, if you join, a mentoring program and access to a research library is included. If you're a quilting historian, this is a group you should join.
- **www.quilt.com** Serving quilters since 1994, this website is a little dated (it hasn't been updated since 2007) but its archives are still worth searching.

Index